CONTENTS

About the Authors

Dr Gráinne Healy holds a PhD from Dublin City University and also a postgraduate qualification in Journalism. A former chairwoman of the National Women's Council of Ireland and Vice-President of the European Women's Lobby, she has worked for twenty years as an independent projects manager. Co-founder of Marriage Equality, she has been its chairwoman since 2008 and was a Co-director of the Yes Equality Campaign.

Brian Sheehan has been centrally involved in the development of LGBT rights and equality nationally for nearly twenty years. Since 2007 he has been the Executive Director of GLEN – the Gay and Lesbian Equality Network one of Ireland's leading LGBT advocacy organisations. Brian works internationally with LGBT human rights organisations in Europe. He was a Co-director of the Yes Equality Campaign.

Noel Whelan is the author and co-author of ten previous books on Irish elections and politics, and most recently co-editor of *Brian Lenihan in Calm and Crisis*, published by Merrion Press in 2014. Noel writes a weekly political column for the *Irish Times* and is a regular commentator for the broadcast media. He works as a barrister, specialising in Criminal and Constitutional Law. He was one of the leaders of the Democracy Matters campaign which successfully opposed the 2013 Seanad Abolition Referendum. He was Strategic Adviser to the Yes Equality Campaign.

Preface

It was with some trepidation that the three of us agreed to write this first-hand account of the Yes Equality referendum campaign. The announcement of the result of the referendum on that sunny Saturday afternoon of 23rd May 2015 was a magical moment in Irish history. The events, campaigns, personal stories, political forces and social factors which shaped that outcome have already been the subject of numerous articles, broadcast discussions and much online commentary. They will inevitably form the basis of many future studies, theses and books. This publication is merely an initial, and inevitably subjective, contribution to the early drafts of the history of that extraordinary campaign.

The Yes Equality campaign was a key factor, although of course not the only key factor, in winning the referendum. Our involvement in the campaign was in coordinating Yes Equality at headquarters level where we were just one part of a large and impressive team. It was an honour to work with such a committed group of people. The headquarters was merely the hub of a massive network of local Yes Equality groups around the country which involved the voluntary effort of thousands of people. It was their contribution which determined the referendum outcome. They led conversations for Yes in their homes, among their social media networks, in workplaces and on hundreds of thousands of doorsteps. This was truly a 'people's referendum'.

Yes Equality has begun a comprehensive project of archiving the campaign. This effort will include detailed interviews with coordinators and activists throughout the country. In due course this archive will shape a definitive historical record of Yes Equality. Seperately Charlie Bird has toured the country to revisit many of those he met during the extraordinary 'I'm Voting Yes Ask Me Why' events which he moderated during the campaign and has gathered their stories for future publication. What we have sought to do in this book is to give recollections of the campaign as it appeared to the three of us. In the space and time available this can only be partial and catches only that which was most prominent in our sight line. Although we were well placed to get an overview of the campaign, we witnessed only a fraction of the incredible activity involved. We can only, for example, scratch the surface of the separate related activities of the partner organisations and political parties who worked with us in this effort.

We must in particular thank the board and staff of GLEN and Marriage Equality, and make a special mention of Mark Kelly and his board and staff at the Irish Council for Civil Liberties (ICCL), who gave so much as volunteers. The successful coalition of these three organisations made Yes Equality possible.

We have sought to summarise some of the journey which gave rise to the referendum, to capture a sense of the overall flavour, excitement and drama of the campaign, to reflect the range and extent of the countrywide effort involved, and to convey the significance of the result.

Those who deserve to be thanked for their work on this campaign are literally innumerable. In the following pages many are mentioned in passing whose contribution deserves much greater recognition, and of necessity there are so many not mentioned at all who know how significant their contribution was. We have sought in the appendices to reflect the individual involvements of those who led the campaign in particular areas or aspects. At the end of the book we have included the speech made by Brian and Gráinne as the Co-directors of Yes Equality on the announcement of the result and have also included the message which Yes Equality Roscommon posted that weekend. These two pieces illustrate the effort involved in Yes Equality and our gratitude at the outcome.

We do want to thank in a special way all those who assisted us with this book.

We are obliged to Conor Graham, Lisa Hyde and all at Merrion Press, who have executed this task with such enthusiasm and flair. The quality of the final production owes much to their efforts. We are grateful to Jonathan Williams, who had the foresight to recognise the wider potential of this book.

Donal Cronin, Séamus Dooley and Kathleen Hunt were kind enough to read the nearly finalised manuscript, to point out some flaws or omissions and to suggest certain additional inclusions or colour. However, any enduring gaps or errors are our responsibility.

A great deal of thanks also goes to Kathryn Marsh, who worked tirelessly and skillfully on the original text to give it greater coherence and to ensure veracity. This was a particular challenge given the tight timescales and the number of authors involved. We are indebted to her for her professionalism and patience.

We would like to acknowledge and thank Paul Sharpe of Sharpix who was official photographer to the campaign. Many of his photos appear in this book. We wish also to thank Steve Humphries at the Irish Independent, Brian Lawless and Peter Morrison of Press Association, Gareth Chaney at Collins Photos, Dara Mac Dónaill at *The Irish Times* and Clodagh Kilcoyne and Paul Faith at Getty Images for use of their photographs. We also thank Dearbhail McDonald, Sebastian Enke, Mark Kelly, Joan Burton TD, Amy Huberman and Carole Ledger for the use of their tweets. We want to say a special thanks to Annie West for her 'Home to Vote' sketch and for permission to reproduce it in this book.

We are touched that, as well as having done so much for the Yes Equality cause, Mary McAleese has also taken the time to write the foreword for this book. We thank her again for her eloquence and passion.

The three of us each wish to thank our families for their support during the campaign itself and again when we further imposed on their patience by agreeing to undertake this book.

Thousands of lives have been changed by this campaign and its outcome. That is due to the people of Ireland. Like so many others, we are profoundly grateful to them for voting in such large numbers for equality.

Gráinne, Brian, Noel
September 2015

Foreword

Mary McAleese

'*Marriage may be contracted in accordance with law by two persons without distinction as to their sex.*'

Adding these seventeen words was an impressive step by the Irish people to insert true equality into our constitution. It marked the final stage in dismantling the centuries old structures, attitudes and beliefs that conduced to homophobia at the heart of our laws. It completed a process that began almost forty years ago when the Campaign for Homosexual Law Reform was established. As a founder member of that campaign, as a lawyer, as a mother and as a citizen I was thrilled and deeply moved that the referendum result was such a definitive Yes.

There are moments in the history of a country that define, reflect and showcase the very best instincts and character of its people. That wonderful weekend last 22nd and 23rd May when Ireland said a resounding Yes to equality for its gay and lesbian citizens was such a moment. Like the overwhelming popular endorsement of the Good Friday Agreement in referendums north and south exactly seventeen years earlier, the result of the marriage referendum showed our respect for the 'otherness of others' and their right to parity of esteem. The marriage equality referendum put beyond doubt the widespread belief in the right of all Irish citizens to live as equals, to love as equals and to marry whoever they choose.

In the most democratic way possible Ireland became the first country in the world to embrace her gay and lesbian children by way of popular referendum. In record numbers Irish voters decided that past branding, stereotyping and isolating of our gay and lesbian citizens was and ever will be unacceptable. The Irish people in their constitution have got their back. For the future wherever homophobia still lurks or raises its ugly voice there will be a large majority to confidently stop it in its tracks.

The result was an occasion for joyous public celebration in the spontaneous carnival that broke out in Dublin Castle and the surrounding streets, and at many other places around the country. It was wonderful for Martin and myself and our family, that sunny afternoon to see the light and happiness on the faces of Yes Equality activists when we joined them in Ballsbridge. They had given so much of themselves during the campaign. Many told their own often harrowing stories on the doorsteps. Sometimes they faced bitter words, sometimes genuine doubt and queries, sometimes understanding and empathy. Their determination and commitment softened hearts, changed many minds and brought the Irish people with them on an amazing journey. By the power of persuasion, by the integrity of their arguments, they won through the war of words, of claim and counter-claim, so that we can face the future now with lighter hearts and greater hopes for our republic and its future generations.

That May weekend of course was also one for many quieter, more private moments of celebration. For families like my own the issue of marriage equality was personal. It was wonderful to be able to celebrate the constitutionally recognised equality our only son can now enjoy. No longer will he be a second-class citizen. Now he has the same marriage rights as his twin and older sister. They and their friends, like thousands of others throughout Ireland, who knocked on doors, gave out leaflets and badges, explained again and again the arguments in favour of marriage equality and countered concerns, can be truly proud of their accomplishments as activists in the Yes Equality campaign. They gave the lie to those who think our young people are disinterested in civic and political affairs. Their infectious passion for equality and fairness was palpable and very, very effective.

The work and approach of the Yes Equality campaign, and of organisations like BeLong To made that grace-filled day in May possible. Those who led the Yes campaign, showed real political skill, and deep insight in framing an upbeat appeal and in recognising the need to persuade and reassure the widest possible audience. They nurtured, supported, co-ordinated, cajoled and encouraged a vast and often spontaneous voluntary effort driven by a love for justice and an abhorrence of unjust discrimination. They created a campaign with a constructive tone and a calm space which enabled many profoundly moving stories about the downstream personal misery caused by intolerance, ignorance and prejudice to be told.

In this book Gráinne, Brian and Noel, who led the campaign to such terrific success, now do the public a further service by sharing their account of the referendum. They tell that story with much of the same mix of enthusiasm and carefulness which marked the campaign itself. In recording the campaign from the Yes perspective they have shared important insights on strategy and methodology. They have shown for example how so much detailed and painstaking work in the months, indeed years, before the referendum, particularly in nurturing groups throughout the country, laid the foundations for the extraordinary surge in online campaigning, family conversation and one-on-one canvassing in the week before polling day. The book also recounts and recognises the range of individual efforts which shaped this important result. I also acknowledge here the men, women and youngsters who did not campaign formally but who became quiet advocates for change in and through tens of thousands of private conversations around dinner tables, in workplaces, colleges, shops, cafes, pubs, streets and wherever two or more were gathered. The Government's decision to advance the referendum and the effort and enthusiasm which they and so many opposition politicians put into the campaign, was also impressive.

There is more to be done, for the work of dismantling the entire architecture of homophobia is still not complete. The achievement of marriage equality surely and irrevocably propelled us further along the road. It lifted some of the intolerable burden our gay and lesbian children have had to carry. It hopefully augurs well for a future where the discovery of a person's sexual orientation will generate optimism and confidence rather than loneliness and worry. The lives of our gay and lesbian citizens and their families, we dearly hope, have been transformed by the outcome of the marriage equality referendum. Our country and its future surely have been. For the better. Thank God.

CHAPTER 1

Constitutional Convention

12th TO 14th APRIL 2013

Poised and elegant, Clare O'Connell stood up to give the most important speech of her life. Her parents, Gráinne and Orla, listened in the viewing room downstairs. Clare began: 'My family is similar to yours. Except for one big difference. My parents are not allowed to get married. My family is not recognised. For the simple reason that my parents are two women.' She had the attention of everyone in the room that Saturday in April 2013 in the Grand Hotel in Malahide in north County Dublin. 'Marriage equality would mean that my parents, who are in a loving and committed relationship, could get married, just like anyone else's parents. But, most importantly for me, marriage equality would mean that no one could ever tell us again that we aren't a family.'

Both Clare O'Connell and Conor Prendergast, who had spoken just before her, electrified the Constitutional Convention. Clearly and passionately, they made real the issue that the Convention was to discuss that weekend. This was no longer an academic, theoretical or legal discussion. This was, in the words of one delegate, 'about real people living real lives as we speak, all across Ireland'. Marriage equality had just taken on a new urgency, and a new familiarity.

The Constitutional Convention was part of the compromise negotiated between Labour and Fine Gael when they formed a coalition government in March 2011. The general election had taken place during a deep economic recession and in the humiliating aftermath of Ireland having to be bailed out by the troika (the IMF, the European Central Bank and the European Commission). Fine Gael had won seventy-six seats, making them the largest party in the Dáil for the first time in the party's history, although they lacked an overall majority. The Labour Party had beaten their previous best, winning thirty-seven seats, to become the second largest party.

The putative coalition partners Fine Gael and Labour, like all of Ireland's political parties, had a record of supporting equality for lesbian and gay people. Labour had been central to the achievement of the decriminalisation of homosexuality and equality legislation, while their private members Civil Union Bill in 2006 was key to building support for subsequent civil partnership legislation. In 2004 Fine Gael had been the first party to publish a proposal for civil unions. Both parties had strongly supported the Civil Partnership Bill introduced by the Fianna Fáil–Green Party government in its passage through the Oireachtas in 2010. Both had made commitments to progress for LGBT people across a range of areas in their election manifestos. Labour pledged to hold a constitutional referendum to bring in marriage for lesbian and gay couples.

Shortly after the election, over the first few days of March 2011, the two parties began intensive negotiations about government formation. Whether marriage equality would be part of the new Programme for Government was touch and go in these discussions.

The document that was eventually agreed upon and published by the two parties focused primarily on repairing the economy and getting people back to work. However, it also included the aim of 'forging a new Ireland that is based on fairness and on equal citizenship' and it promised to establish a Constitutional Convention which, within twelve months, would consider and make recommendations on six specific issues, including 'provision for same-sex marriage'.

It took until July 2012 to finally set up the Convention, which was established by a resolution of both Houses of the Oireachtas. Tom Arnold, then Chief Executive of the development charity Concern Worldwide and a respected public figure, was subsequently appointed to chair it. The Convention had 100 members. In addition to Arnold, there were sixty-six people who were randomly selected members of the public and thirty-three people who were elected members of either the Oireachtas or the Northern Ireland Assembly. The first meeting of the Constitutional Convention was in December 2012, and in 2013 they met for a weekend almost every month to discuss and vote on one of the allotted topics.

The Convention was scheduled to discuss 'same-sex marriage' in April 2013. For lesbian and gay people and their families, this was a critical moment. Rejection would set the campaign back years; a recommendation for constitutional change would create a momentum that it would be hard to halt. It was a moment to define what the Irish Republic could become.

Three of the LGBT members of the Oireachtas, Jerry Buttimer TD, John Lyons TD and Senator Katherine Zappone, were delegates to the Convention and several of the other Oireachtas members of the convention were also strong supporters of marriage equality. These included Frances Fitzgerald TD, Charlie Flanagan TD, Aódhan Ó Ríordáin TD, Mary Lou McDonald TD and Senators Averil Power and Susan O'Keeffe. One of the main opponents of marriage equality, Senator Ronan Mullen, was also a delegate. The debates that eventually played out across the stage of the referendum campaign were solidly rehearsed at the Convention.

The Convention had settled on a format for each of its weekends. On Saturday mornings an expert panel gave delegates an overview of the legal and constitutional context of whatever issue was being discussed. Then representatives from each side made their case to the whole Convention in plenary session before the delegates deliberated in small groups at their tables. Later, each table group reported back to a plenary session and then a question and answer period was held with a balanced panel of stakeholders. On Sunday morning the delegates, having reflected on the issue overnight, debated the wording of the precise recommendation to government on which they would vote. Then they voted on the proposal and the result of the vote was announced.

The Convention secretariat, which was led by an able civil servant, Art O'Leary, proposed that the Gay and Lesbian Equality Network (GLEN), Marriage Equality, and the Irish Council for Civil Liberties (ICCL) would make presentations on one side, and that the Irish Catholic Bishops' Conference, the Knights of Colombanus and the Evangelical Association of Ireland would present on the other.[1]

In March 2013 the Convention secretariat invited GLEN, Marriage Equality and the ICCL to a meeting to discuss the format for the April weekend and told them that, in all, they would have thirty minutes to address the delegates. It was at that stage that the three organisations agreed to join forces and develop a combined pitch that would play to their respective strengths.

GLEN had been campaigning for full legal and constitutional equality for lesbian, gay and bisexual people since 1988. Marriage Equality had been campaigning and raising public and political awareness on the issue since forming to support a High Court case taken by Katherine Zappone and Ann Louise Gilligan in 2004 to have their Canadian marriage recognised in Ireland. The ICCL had been a long-time champion of gay rights over much of its forty-year history.

The Convention secretariat had received more than 1,000 submissions on marriage equality, which was the highest number they received on any topic. They used these submissions to identify the core issues on which the external experts prepared papers, which were then presented on that Saturday morning in April 2013.

Gerry Durcan SC began by outlining the current position of marriage and the family in the Constitution. He was followed by barrister Dr Eimer Browne, who outlined the provisions for legal recognition of relationships and families for lesbian and gay couples, and highlighted the growing trend internationally to recognise same-sex relationships as being equivalent, or very near, to marriage. Dr Sarah Fennell, also a barrister, then focused on the legislative change that would be necessary if marriage equality was permitted and highlighted adoption, parenting and guardianship as key issues for change. The last to speak on this panel was Professor Jim Sheehan, an expert in family therapy, who discussed the findings from studies across the world that explored the outcomes for children who had grown up in households with lesbian or gay parents. He concluded that, although there were no firm conclusions, most research failed to suggest adverse effects.

The issues of parenting and children were to emerge as contentious throughout the weekend. The Iona Institute, a Roman Catholic think-tank that 'promotes the place of marriage and religion in society', in its submission to the Convention had quoted research, entitled *Marriage from a Child's Perspective: How Does Family Structure Affect Children, and What Can We Do about It?* published by the Washington-based Child Trends research centre in 2002. Iona claimed 'the research demonstrates why a truly child-centred society will continue to give marriage between a man and a woman special status and will not see this as unfair and unjustified discrimination'. The authors of the research had, however, included a strong disclaimer, saying that the research did not include same-sex or adoptive parents. On hearing that the Iona Institute had cited their study, the authors had actually written to the Convention to ensure that their research was not used as an argument against marriage equality.

Once the experts had explained the context to the delegates, GLEN, the ICCL and Marriage Equality made their presentation. They asked the Convention 'to recommend to Government to provide for equal access to marriage for same-sex couples in the Constitution'. They spoke of the way in which Irish people had increasingly supported extensions of equal rights and legal protections over the previous twenty years. They pointed out how two years of civil partnerships had dramatically increased the visibility of lesbian and gay couples across every county in Ireland, enabling increasing numbers of people to see that the love and commitment of a lesbian or gay couple was the same as that of a heterosexual couple. This had contributed to a growing momentum for equality of relationship recognition. They spoke about the nature of citizenship in the Republic of Ireland and what that might mean for constitutional change. They talked about children in families with gay or lesbian parents and how civil partnership did not recognise them. They explained that these existing families across the country urgently needed protection and recognition. They spoke also about the emerging human rights case for marriage equality and about the positive social impact in those countries where equal marriage was already in place. They pointed to the strong support among the Irish public for marriage equality. Above all else, they emphasised the desire of lesbian and gay people all over Ireland to be treated equally, to become full and equal citizens. They showed delegates a short film by film maker Linda Cullen that featured couples, young and old, male and female, with and without children, who asked for equal recognition for their relationships and families.

It was Clare and Conor, however, who transformed these solid rational arguments into flesh and blood and brought home to the delegates exactly why their parents wanted to be able to marry. Both had become advocates through the Believe in Equality project by Marriage Equality, which worked with children of lesbian and gay couples. Conor compared himself to his parents, Ann and Bernadette. 'I'm lucky enough now to be engaged myself, which for us is obviously wonderful, but it is bittersweet. I've been with my fiancée Alanna for six years, but my parents have been together for thirty-two years. Yet they can't have their love recognised by marriage. And that's what marriage is for really. About recognising love,' said Conor. 'I don't want to face a future where my parents are older and the caring shoe is on the other foot and where I'm not recognised as their son. As their legal next of kin,' he added.

There was a fierce round of applause for Conor as he finished.

The bishops were the next to speak. It wasn't the first time they had spoken against equality for gay people and it wouldn't be the last. Bishop Leo O'Reilly began by quoting Jean Valjean from *Les Misérables* by Victor Hugo: 'To love another person is to see the face of God.' Married love, he said, 'was a unique form of love which was of special benefit and a fundamental building block of society. Changing that would have huge and long-term implications for our country and our children.' This suggestion of unforeseen consequences if marriage equality was allowed was a constant refrain for the next two days. It was best answered by one delegate who said that maybe the Convention should focus on the foreseen and happy consequences; that lesbian and gay couples would be able to marry.

Bishop O'Reilly talked of love representing a fundamental part of being a Christian, saying that love demanded respect and dignity for every human being. He explained that this was 'why the Catholic Church insists that people who are homosexual should be treated with sensitivity, compassion, respect'. One delegate later said that the arguments of the No side were couched in language that should have come from the Yes side. Words like 'mutual respect, compassion, dignity', if they were meant, would surely lead one to support marriage equality.

Bishop O'Reilly, left it to Breda McDonald from the Irish Catholic Bishops' Conference Council for Marriage and the Family to deal with the issue of children. Her main point was that since marriage 'opened up the possibility of children' and lesbian or gay couples cannot bring a child into the world themselves, marriage should be restricted to opposite-sex couples. 'Are we,' Breda asked, 'to be the first generation in human history to be asked if the roles of mothers and fathers are to be consigned to history and considered irrelevant in the bringing up of children?'

Bishop O'Reilly, Breda McDonald, and after them the Knights of Columbanus spoke on many of the issues that would later form the basis of the No arguments in the referendum. Even though they lacked evidential foundations, their arguments raised doubts about the wisdom of changing the *status quo*. They suggested that people would be labelled as being opposed to fundamental rights if they 'resisted the redefinition of marriage'; that there would be a rupture between Northern Ireland and the Republic if marriage equality came in; that a radical redefinition of marriage was not necessary to resolve the grievances of same-sex couples; and that freedom of religion and conscience could not be protected if equal marriage was introduced.

After the groups had made their presentations, the private sessions at individual tables allowed the claims by both sides to be fully interrogated. The team advocating for marriage equality waited nervously in the viewing room downstairs; their nervousness was shared by the thousands of LGBT people who were watching the live online relay of the public sessions. Indeed, such was the level of interest in the deliberations of the Constitutional Convention among the LGBT community that hundreds gathered that Saturday and Sunday in Pantibar, a prominent Dublin city centre gay bar, to watch the live broadcast of proceedings on large screens.

The key points of the delegates' discussions at each table were reported back in the next session. It was clear that Clare and Conor had made a profound impact. Many delegates stated that children need equality regardless of sexual orientation of parents or the nature of their relationship and moved from that principled position to supporting marriage equality. The arguments of those opposed had hit home for some though. 'Unforeseen consequences' was a key issue, along with fears that not enough was known about the impact of marriage equality and that its introduction should wait. Questions were raised about the main purpose of marriage, which some felt was to produce children, and thus was distinct and separate and so should not be available to lesbian and gay couples. There were fears that existing and future marriages between opposite-sex couples would somehow be diminished. For the first time, surrogacy emerged as an issue.

After the delegates had reported back, there was another wide-ranging discussion in plenary session. One delegate noted that the bishops did not represent the views of the many Christians in the room who supported marriage equality. Charlie Flanagan TD and others talked about how traditional marriage had witnessed huge change over the years, with greater fairness, justice and equality within marriage, particularly for women. Senator Ronan Mullen raised three questions that he was to repeat several times during the weekend: whether more time was needed to understand the implications of what was being proposed, particularly on matters like adoption and assisted human reproduction; whether issues such as guardianship and anti-bullying measures could be tackled through legislation rather than Constitutional change; and, if an amendment was recommended, how would latitude be given to legislators to nuance the issues to protect the freedom of those who disagreed with marriage equality or the extension of adoption and assisted human reproduction. To advocates of marriage equality who were listening and watching, it was ironic that Senator Mullen was proposing legislative progress for lesbian and gay people, given that he was one of only four members of both Houses of the Oireachtas to vote against the Civil Partnership Bill in 2010.

The next panel included David Quinn, who as well as being an *Irish Independent* columnist, was director of the Iona Institute. Quinn said that it was not discrimination to treat different things differently, that complementarity of the sexes means that only men and women could be married, and that while circumstances sometimes lead to children being raised without their biological parents, if same-sex couples were allowed to marry, this would be the first time that the state would 'deliberately deprive a child of its natural mother and father'.

Also on the panel was Colm O'Gorman, Director of Amnesty International Ireland, who challenged Quinn, saying that treating people differently in law was permissible only where there is an objective reason for doing so.

Joining them on the panel was Conor O'Mahony, a constitutional law lecturer in University College Cork. He emphasised that 'preventing gay couples from marrying does not prevent children from being brought up by same-sex couples', and that it was very difficult to see any impacts on opposite-sex couples from a legal or social point of view if lesbian and gay couples could marry.

The fourth panellist, Michael Dwyer, was from the Preserve Marriage organisation. Dwyer was a gay man who opposed marriage equality. He said that his view of marriage was not that it was a statement of love between adults but that it was an institution that had 'evolved socially for the protection of children'. He said that the State should privilege one form of family as the 'aspirational form of family' and should support that as the ideal through the tax codes and other legislation.

Stephen Agnew from the Alliance Party, who was one of the Northern Ireland delegates to the Convention, said: 'If you accepted the research findings showing marriage as the best environment for children, why would you not ensure that the disadvantaged children get all the advantages available? Why would you withhold the advantages of marriage from them?'

Senator Averil Power noted that all the main children's organisations supported the principle of children being treated equally and supported marriage equality because it is good for children. 'Why,' she asked, 'would we discriminate against good and happy families?'

O'Gorman then spoke emotionally about his family. 'I'm a man married to a man and I have children,' he started. 'For lots of reasons over the last twenty years I've regularly stood up and talked about intimate parts of my life because I believe it's been important to public discourse in my society. And it's not always been easy. I'm really tired of doing it. Really, really tired.' He described the regular daily life with his husband and their two children. 'I love my children and my children love me. And what I would like more than anything else from this Republic, my Republic, is that we would be treated with respect and regard and be celebrated like every other family who in their flawed, unique way tries to get through their life as best as they possibly can.' There was a stillness in the room after his speech.

Michael Dwyer intervened to raise issues from a Canadian police force report which, he said, talked about heightened levels of abuse in stepparent families and claimed that 'children living in step families were 120 times more likely to be killed than those living with their biological parents'. Challenged by Senator Susan O'Keeffe, he stated that he was not saying that gay people hadn't the capacity to be parents, but he continued to quote research about poverty and the incidence of violence in step families. Asked by the chair, Tom Arnold, to clarify the situation, psychologist Jim Sheehan dismissed Dwyer's claims, saying that the research Dwyer was quoting related only to opposite-sex parenting families and was nothing to do with marriage for same-sex couples. David Quinn then challenged what he described as the emotional presentations of Clare O'Connell and Conor Prendergast.

The Convention concluded for the day, and when proceedings recommenced on Sunday they began with a discussion by the delegates on the wording of proposals to go to Government. The debate over the next hour and a half was particularly tense.

Fears of unintended consequences were raised frequently. In a foretaste of what was to come in the final days of the referendum, there was a series of proposals from the floor to add civil partnership to the Constitution, with the same rights and obligations as marriage. Senator Zappone challenged that view robustly, saying that, even if such a provision gave equal rights to same-sex couples, it was still exclusionary. It was a lesser form of acknowledgement of same-sex relationships and was rooted in a principle which promoted inequality. Lesbian and gay couples would still be excluded from the socially valuable institution of marriage.

Senator Mullen again raised the issue of protection of freedom of religion and expression of such beliefs, and the protections necessary to ensure that those individuals and institutions who believed that marriage was only between a man and a woman could express that view. He asked that provisions be included so that the legislature could restrict assisted human reproduction to heterosexual couples if it so wished. He wanted to have a freedom of conscience clause to protect people from unintended consequences that might prevent, for example, schools from teaching their vision of marriage as defined by their religious ethos. Many delegates pointed out that such a provision had not been included when divorce had been brought in by constitutional amendment, and this had not caused a problem for schools.

Listening to this at the back of the room and in the viewing room downstairs, GLEN, Marriage Equality and the ICCL could see that Mullen's trenchant style was having an impact. They were seriously concerned that he would sway delegates to oppose reform. The mood in the room had changed. The idea of putting civil partnership in the Constitution had taken hold.

It was at this precise moment that John Lyons TD and Jerry Buttimer TD each made powerful and emotional interventions and brought the discussion back from intellectual debate to what they both considered to be the core of the issue: their lives, their love and their desire to be equal citizens. 'Anything less than full civil marriage for every single individual is discrimination. Call it anything else, but it is discrimination. And if you're happy to discriminate against people that's your prerogative, but I'm not happy to discriminate against anyone in this Republic and I ask you to remember that today,' said Lyons.

Buttimer made a direct and personal appeal to delegates. 'I hope you've never felt that we're attacking you or disrespected your viewpoint. It is because I saw my parents' marriage that I value and cherish marriage. I want to marry the person I love to enhance and enrich my life. Love between two people should never be undermined.'

The proposal to vote on adding civil partnership as a distinct entity to the Constitution was eventually dismissed by the chairman, who said that the express request from the Houses of the Oireachtas to the Convention was that they should discuss a proposal on whether or not to include same-sex marriage in the Constitution. Mullen's proposal of additional wording for the delegates to vote to allow 'individuals, families and institutions to espouse their preferred understanding of marriage' and to allow the State to 'make appropriate distinctions in order to ensure the best interests of children' was rejected as being unclear and full of unforeseen consequences. Gerry Durcan SC asked whether this would mean that people who believed in polygamous marriage should be entitled to have this recognised by the State.

All discussions were now over and the delegates began to vote. GLEN, Marriage Equality and the ICCL, observing at the back of the room, were asked to leave. Those following online and on social media began a nervous wait. The crowd in Pantibar fell quiet.

An hour later the results were announced. They were extraordinary: 79 out of 100 delegates voted to ask the Government to change the Constitution to allow for civil marriage for same-sex couples. In an even more surprising result, 81 out of 100 delegates voted for changing the laws around parenting, guardianship and the upbringing of children to equally include children in lesbian and gay headed families.

Pantibar erupted. Downstairs at the Grand Hotel in Malahide, many from the three organisations wept. Something momentous had been achieved. GLEN, ICCL and Marriage Equality held their first joint press conference to welcome the outcome as a historic day and a major milestone on the journey to full constitutional equality for lesbian and gay people, and families, in Ireland.

The next step was to persuade the Government to hold a referendum.

CHAPTER 2

Yes Equality: A Campaign is Born

MAY 2013 TO MARCH 2015

Having worked so closely and so successfully on their joint presentation for the Constitutional Convention, the leaders of GLEN, Marriage Equality and ICCL quickly began to think about how they could work together not only to ensure that the Government would agree to hold a referendum but also to build a combined campaigning organisation to deliver a victory for marriage in such a referendum.

The three organisations now had one common objective and focus, namely the passing of a constitutional amendment to extend to same-sex couples the right to marry. They came to work well together in achieving that objective. That they managed to do so was far from inevitable. Indeed, the very idea of them cooperating in this joint enterprise surprised many who were familiar with their different organisational histories and the earlier tensions between Marriage Equality and GLEN, in particular around the issue of civil partnership.

GLEN had been established in 1988 by a group of gay and lesbian activists, led by Kieran Rose and Christopher Robson, to focus on delivering legal and social equality for lesbian, gay and bisexual people.

They had a clear and ambitious vision, despite the climate of fear driven by the AIDS crisis. Their aims were to have LGBT people no longer considered criminals, ensure full protection in the workplace and in accessing goods and services, and have their relationships and families recognised and protected. Their first success was the achievement of decriminalisation of homosexuality in 1993, following on from Senator David Norris's winning case in the European Court.

This was quickly followed by a range of other transformative changes, most notably workplace equality for lesbian and gay people in 1998, and full protection in the provision of goods and services in 2000. GLEN then turned its attention to achieving equal recognition and protection of lesbian and gay relationships and families. Political parties became increasingly supportive; however, talk of a possible constitutional barrier also began to emerge. GLEN, with expanded staff numbers following an investment by The Atlantic Philanthropies, stepped up its efforts. A pivotal political moment occurred in 2006 when the Colley Report was published by the Minister for Justice Michael McDowell, which stated that the only option that guaranteed full equality for lesbian and gay couples was marriage. Eoin Collins from GLEN was a member of that working group. By this stage, all political parties had come to the view that marriage would require a constitutional referendum.

In 2008 the Fianna Fáil–Green Party government published a Civil Partnership Bill. This included almost all of the legal rights and obligations of civil marriage, although it was not marriage and did not have constitutional protection. Critically, the outline was silent on children in lesbian and gay-headed families. While GLEN did not agree that a referendum was necessary to achieve marriage, it nevertheless supported the civil partnership proposals, seeing it as providing urgently needed protections. They also believed that the visibility of lesbian and gay couples having civil partnerships would radically alter the perception of lesbian and gay relationships, and would be an important catalyst for marriage and family recognition. GLEN then began the intense political involvement necessary to secure the passage of the Civil Partnership Bill, which eventually passed all stages in the Oireachtas in July 2010. The GLEN board and staff enhanced their engagement with political parties and the public to build the appetite for marriage.

Marriage equality, as the name suggests, has always been the sole organisational goal of Marriage Equality. The group was set up originally as a support group called KAL in 2004 when Katherine Zappone and Ann Louise Gilligan were given leave to appeal a decision by the Revenue Commissioners which refused to recognise their Canadian marriage. This group transformed into Marriage Equality in 2008 and its founding chairpersons were Gráinne Healy and Denise Charlton. In that year Moninne Griffith, a solicitor, was recruited as the organisation's full-time director. She created a team that included Dawn Quinn as administrator and Kirsten Foster, who worked on communications. In 2009 Andrew Hyland, who had worked with the group as a communications consultant, joined the team as co-director with Moninne. With support from the marriage equality movement in the United States, Marriage Equality in Ireland devised a strategic plan. A key component of this was an 'Out to Your TD' campaign, which involved gay and lesbian people and their families visiting the clinics of their local politicians to persuade them to support marriage equality. This was backed by a communications strategy which focused on raising the profile of LGBT couples and their families and giving their children a voice. This work, in the words of Brian Finnegan, editor of *Gay Community News*, was instrumental in making 'marriage equality a popular movement in Ireland'. Marriage Equality was also active in speaking to and answering questions from politicians and civil servants concerning the issue. Marriage Equality saw the gaps in parenting rights and recognitions in Civil Partnership as intolerable and unequal. Meanwhile, the LGBT community generally was increasingly demanding full civil marriage equality and Gráinne, Moninne and their colleagues saw an urgent need for the organisations to work together to achieve this.

The ICCL also had a long history of working on these issues. In 1990 the ICCL had convened a Working Party on Lesbian and Gay

Rights. This group included ICCL's Tom Cooney, and Kieran Rose and Christopher Robson of GLEN. In the immediate aftermath of the Norris judgement against Ireland by the European Court of Human Rights in 1988, this working group produced a ground-breaking report, *Equality Now for Lesbians and Gay Men*, which charted the discrimination and prejudice to which lesbian and gay people were subjected and recommended various solutions to the problem. The report significantly influenced the legislation decriminalising homosexuality which was ultimately introduced by Máire Geoghegan-Quinn TD and Minister for Justice in 1993.

Mark Kelly, a human rights lawyer, became ICCL director in 2006, at which time the work had just finished on an ICCL publication, *Equality for All Families*, which concluded that same-sex couples should no longer be barred from entering civil marriage. Kelly was anxious to support Zappone and Gilligan in their case and was determined that the ICCL and Marriage Equality would begin to forge strong working relationships. While differing on whether or not civil partnership would lead to civil marriage, ICCL always shared a commitment to the ultimate goal of full marriage equality.

When the need to work together became clear, Gráinne Healy, Chairwoman of Marriage Equality, was not only finishing a doctorate in Dublin City University but also taking a more active voluntary executive role in Marriage Equality. Shortly after the Constitutional Convention she decided to invite Mark Kelly of ICCL and Brian Sheehan of GLEN to meet to discuss the next steps. This began a pattern of fortnightly post-Convention planning sessions between the three organisations that intensified to become weekly meetings once the holding of a referendum was announced.

The most immediate tasks when these meetings began in the middle of 2013 centred on securing a formal government commitment to hold the referendum, having the government publicly identify a date for that referendum and shaping the legislative reform around children and family rights which would precede the referendum proposal.

By the autumn of 2013 government sources were suggesting to the media that they would accept the recommendations of the

Constitutional Convention to hold a referendum and that they would first enact the family law reform legislation. It was also made known that Alan Shatter TD, the Minister for Justice and Equality, and a leading family law expert, was personally drafting a Children and Family Relationships Bill, which, as well as providing for a range of modernisations of family law generally, would address almost all the issues for lesbian and gay headed families with children.

In October 2013 Tánaiste Eamon Gilmore confirmed that a referendum on marriage equality would be held either in 2014 or in the spring of 2015. A few weeks later, on 5th November, the Cabinet made a formal decision and announced that a referendum would be held in 2015. GLEN, ICCL and Marriage Equality together welcomed this announcement.

Minister Shatter also obtained Cabinet approval that day for his Children and Family Relationships Bill, and published details of its proposed content in a comprehensive briefing note.

It was clear that the legislation as proposed would give much-needed recognition and protection to gay and lesbian headed households. While they had warmly welcomed the promised referendum, GLEN and Marriage Equality decided to maintain a low public profile in relation to the Children and Family Relationships Bill. They took a view that the wide-ranging reforms reflected in the proposed legislation were needed for all types of families and a focus on same-sex headed families might delay its passage. Children's and family rights organisations warmly welcomed the proposals and GLEN, Marriage Equality and ICCL decided that they would work closely with them, and with Minister Shatter and his department, on the detail of the legislation.

At the Government press conference that November evening, the Taoiseach, Enda Kenny, spoke strongly of his support for marriage equality and promised that he would campaign actively for a Yes vote in the upcoming referendum. The tenor of his public remarks was significant in underlining the Government's support for the legislation and carried an important message to his own party members in Fine Gael. With the leader of every political party now actively supporting marriage equality, mainstream political support for a No vote was unlikely to emerge.

A few weeks later Minister Shatter published the Heads of Bill setting out the detailed provisions of the Children and Family Relationships Bill, and in January 2014 the Joint Oireachtas Committee on Justice began pre-legislative hearings on it. GLEN, Marriage Equality and ICCL again coordinated their submissions to the Joint Oireachtas Committee and made oral presentations. Among those who made submissions in opposition to the Bill was a new organisation called Mothers and Fathers Matter, which had been established to campaign against the proposed legislation. Their spokespersons at the committee hearing included Dr Tom Finnegan, an academic specialising in law and philosophy who had been a parliamentary researcher to Senator Ronan Mullen. The provisions providing for the regulation of surrogacy that Minister Shatter had included in the Bill were the focus of many of the presentations and discussions at the committee.

For the first five months of 2014, however the Department of Justice and Equality was consumed with a range of policing and criminal justice controversies which also dominated the news and political agenda. On 7th May 2014 the Minister, Alan Shatter, resigned. While frustrated at the implications this political turmoil was having for the pace of government preparations for the referendum, the organisations were happy that the new Justice Minister was Frances Fitzgerald TD, who had until then been Minister for Children and who had been another long-time supporter of equality for LGBT people. There was every confidence that, although the time frame would be extended, the complex bill and the referendum would proceed.

In September 2014 Minister Fitzgerald published a revised Heads of Bill, which dropped the proposal to regulate surrogacy but retained most of the provisions that mattered to lesbian and gay families. The bill, while not seen as perfect, would still be of enormous benefit to many families, although the omission of surrogacy made it more likely that this would be a hot topic during the referendum campaign itself. As it happened, the Children and Family Relations Bill was not finalised until early 2015 and was not enacted by the Oireachtas until weeks before the referendum campaign properly began. This was not the timing Yes campaigners had hoped for.

There was another development in the first half of 2014 that gave advocates for marriage equality a jolt.

On the 11th of January 2014, the drag artist and gay rights activist Rory O'Neill appeared on RTÉ television's *The Saturday Night Show*, talking about what it felt like to be gay in Ireland. He said that, despite the positive change in attitude toward gay people, there remained some, particularly in the public eye, who were 'really horrible and mean about gays'. Prompted by the host of the show, Brendan O'Connor, to name them, a slightly hesitant Rory mentioned several columnists who wrote in national newspapers and referred to the Iona Institute. He explained what he meant by homophobia, how all of us are 'a little bit homophobic' in the same way as we are all 'a little bit racist', that it came from our upbringing, from an Ireland that had been isolated and inward-looking and didn't know or understand much about difference, and that we had an inherent bias or maybe prejudice against people who were not the same as us. To most LGBT people watching, he articulated something they all felt was real. To many others, he seemed to be opening a door to an experience of being Irish that they had not known about before.

All hell broke loose. Within a few days some of the columnists who were named and individuals connected with the Iona Institute sued RTÉ for libel and defamation. RTÉ paid €75,000 to settle the claims, removed the clip from the online RTÉ Player and made an apology on the programme two weeks later.

The ensuing controversy, which became known as 'Pantigate', began a debate in Ireland about how people spoke about and behaved towards lesbian and gay people. The discussions raged on social media, on TV, radio and in print; the issue was raised in both the Irish and European parliaments. A large protest was held in Dublin against RTÉ's decision. To many, it felt as if the possibility of a real debate about the experience of being LGBT was closed down. How could you have a debate without naming what you were talking about, what you were experiencing daily, as homophobia? The barrister and columnist Noel Whelan, then unassociated with the campaign, wrote in the *Irish Times,* raising concerns about those in favour of marriage equality using terms that were harsh and potent and which alienated people. He wrote that 'in their anxiety to advance the issue of gay rights, some liberals indeed are seeking to set aside the basic tenets of free speech' and that his worry 'at this early stage of the campaign is that the intolerance shown by some liberal advocates on the issue will undermine the prospects of achieving constitutional reform'.

Three weeks after his *Saturday Night Show* appearance, Rory, this time as his alter-ego Miss Panti Bliss, was invited to give 'The Noble Call' on the stage of the Abbey Theatre at the end of *The Risen People*, a play about the 1913 Lockout. His speech from the stage was a remarkable, articulate and raw exposition of how it feels to be a gay person in Ireland, and it immediately went viral. It was a searingly honest account of how LGBT people had been made to feel unequal and not valued by the society they grew up in and live in. He spoke movingly about how that felt. He spoke of the oppression he himself felt when, in order to avoid harassment, he checked himself at pedestrian crossings to see 'what gave the gay away', and how he hated himself for doing that. He called himself homophobic.

Panti talked about 'nice people, respectable people, smart people, who write for newspapers, having a reasoned debate about you' on TV panels, who all felt it was totally acceptable and reasonable to have a debate about what rights you deserve 'about what kind of person you are, about whether you are capable of being a good parent, of whether you want to destroy marriage, about whether you are safe around children'. Rory named this as homophobia, saying:

'So now Irish gay people find themselves in the ludicrous situation where not only are we not allowed to say publicly what we feel oppressed by, we're not even allowed to think it. Because our definition has been disallowed by our betters.'

'... the word homophobia is no longer available to gay people. Which is a spectacular and neat Orwellian trick because now it turns out that gay people are not the victims of homophobia; homophobes are.'

'Almost all of you are probably homophobes, but I'm a homophobe. To grow up in a society that is overwhelmingly and stiflingly homophobic and to somehow escape unscathed would be miraculous.'

Again and again Yes campaigners were to be charged with labelling those opposed to marriage equality as homophobic, which allowed the key advocates of a No vote to talk of the oppressed, silent No majority who were too afraid to speak out. It is debatable whether 'Pantigate' contributed to or detracted from the early stages of the pre-referendum debate among the broader public. Many may not have heard what was being said. However, Panti's words from the Abbey stage had a galvanising effect on LGBT people and their allies.

The video of Panti's 'Noble Call' was viewed almost a million times. It encapsulated the experience of LGBT people in many different countries and has inspired LGBT activists around the globe.

While the Pantigate controversy provided a backdrop for early discussion about the referendum, GLEN, Marriage Equality and the ICCL were already engaged in early planning for the full campaign. The leadership and executive staff of the three organisations were meeting weekly. Although these meetings focused on the progress of the legislation and the coverage of related issues, they increasingly began to lay down the organisational foundations for the referendum campaign itself. The meetings spent much time discussing how the new campaign should be structured, what activity it should focus on, and they inevitably spent too much time discussing what the new campaigning entity should be called.

Conscious of suggestions from polls that the public needed to be reassured that religious marriage was not going to be affected, they finally settled on the clunky working title 'The Campaign for Civil

Marriage Equality'. All involved, however, realised that the naming and positioning of the Yes campaign would ultimately be shaped by the overall design and look adopted. They decided to seek ideas on this from some of the most innovative design and advertising outfits in the country. By July a request to tender was devised for the brand, which included the design of the initial literature and the related website. Five companies were invited to present. The brief was to create an identity that was 'iconic, creates talkability, is dynamic, dignified but eye catching, inspires and is simple'. It had to be a design that would 'energise and inspire the public imagination and engage people across all ages' in the proposed marriage equality referendum. A special group was established to assess the presentations, comprising Natalie Weadick, the co-chair of GLEN, Brian Sheehan, Walter Jayawardene, Communications Officer with ICCL, Andrew Hyland and Orla Howard from Marriage Equality, who had a background in media buying.

Adam May made their job easy. The presentations were all scheduled to be held at ICCL's offices in Blackhall Place over one day in early August 2014. Adam and his company, Language, were the second group to present.

Like a showman teasing his audience, Adam talked of the company's background on social justice campaigns over many years, while Diarmuid MacAonghusa from Fusio, their web design partners, showed some of their work.

Then came the reveal. Adam put up a large card showing the design and name they were suggesting for the new organisation: *Yes Equality. The Campaign for Civil Marriage Equality* and then one better: *Tá Comhionannas: Feachtas Do Pósadh Sibhialta*. He then showed several executions of the design idea.

At that moment the campaign identity that the three groups had been striving to visualise was born. There it was, as a badge that was to become iconic, in a typeface that was to be adopted and used all over the world. "Yes Equality" looked and felt right. It did not identify the campaign as lesbian, or gay, or LGBT, but identified it as the collective values of Irish people. It would not be about 'them'

– lesbian and gay couples, isolated, apart from, not fully integrated with their broader families and communities. This campaign would create an identity in which everyone could see themselves and the values they would be happy to stand up and vote for. "Yes Equality" did just that. With minor changes to the colour scheme to include more primary colours, the campaign identity that would inspire and energise was now live.

Adam and his team had included a tag line: 'It's time ... for a more inclusive Ireland; for change; for a more equal Ireland.' That felt somewhat pushy. Irish people would be the ones to decide if it was indeed time. The hesitation centred on tone. The campaign would have to make sure that it was not perceived as hectoring or as harassing people into voting Yes. Many knew that the opposition would attempt to paint themselves as victims of a minority group of gay people and of the liberal, biased media who were seeking to hoodwink Irish people and radically change Ireland, suppressing voices opposed to change.

Now that they had a common name to go with their common purpose, Yes Equality began to work on a number of initiatives that would help build capacity and cement relationships for the wider campaign effort. The most important of these was the Register to Vote initiative it launched in the autumn of 2014.

In July 2014, Brian had drawn up a proposal for the three organisations to use the annual November voter registration window to remind voters that the referendum was expected the following year and to build on the work already being done to raise awareness on the issue of marriage equality. The main targets for the registration effort were those under forty years of age, and more particularly those under twenty-five who were not yet registered to vote, or who were registered but hadn't realised the importance of casting their vote.

Voter turnout in the younger age-groups had traditionally been poor – only 19 per cent of those under twenty-five had voted in the Seanad referendum in October 2013. A study by the National Youth Council of Ireland, published in September 2014, had shown that 30 per cent of the same age-group were not registered to vote, while just over half of those who were registered had actually voted in the previous May's Local and European elections. The forthcoming marriage equality referendum therefore provided an exciting opportunity to engage younger people in direct democracy.

The three organisations realised that this registration initiative would be a way to frame their referendum campaign. They would not have the resources or infrastructure of a political party to mount a national referendum campaign on their own, but they could use the Register to Vote initiative to empower organisations and people to be the campaign themselves. They needed to persuade younger people that registering to vote was not about continuing politics as usual; they wanted them to realise that the upcoming referendum was a key generational moment where they could become agents of the change they wished to see. It was also an important moment to set a positive, engaging and vibrant tone. They saw the potential for this to become the largest voter registration campaign ever seen in the State. Social media was going to be critical in reaching the intended audience and that would mean using strategies and tactics not seen before in Irish politics.

In August 2014 liaisons between the three organisations were formalised by the creation of a steering group, which initially comprised Brian, Gráinne and Mark Kelly, with senior staff who met regularly to oversee both structural, financial and governing matters for the embryonic campaign. In early September the Register to Vote plan was signed off at one of their regular meetings. The campaign would focus solely on voter registration. It would not advocate a Yes vote. Tiernan Brady took the lead in implementing the initiative. Tiernan was policy director with GLEN and had played a key role in working with the political parties on the Civil Partnership legislation. He was also a former Fianna Fáil mayor of Bundoran and had a wide range of political contacts.

Everyone was feeling their way very gingerly. The Register to Vote effort would help build a new brand, bringing together the three organisations, yet forging a separate entity from them. The

Yes Equality branding from Language was a terrific starting point. It gave them a confident, upbeat and warm identity. It now had to be tailored for initial use in the registration initiative. That execution also had to be upbeat, engaging, universal and adaptable by all those who would need to be involved in rolling it out. Adam suggested a colour splash as the design execution for Register to Vote. It conveyed movement, energy and excitement and was overlaid with 'Yes Equality'. Everyone in the wider coalition knew it was exactly right. It stayed away from the rainbow used so often for gay issues, but transformed the energy of those primary colours.

In preparation for launching Register to Vote, there were early discussions with existing marriage equality partner organisations such as BeLonG To and the Union of Students in Ireland (USI) in which each saw the potential in a mass campaign and were anxious to support it. The USI president was Laura Harmon, who had been a long-time volunteer in the Cork branch of Marriage Equality. USI always ran an annual voter registration drive and when approached, Laura and USI vice-president for Equality Annie Hoey, immediately offered to integrate their campaign with the one being put in place by Yes Equality. BeLonG To agreed to promote voter registration across their national network of youth workers and through their contacts in youth work throughout Ireland. The trade unions also came on board for the Register to Vote initiative. Andrew was working with USI and Moninne was closely liaising with BeLonG To.

In early October the Register to Vote team met all the LGBT community groups to outline the plan. They were delighted. It offered them a means to harness the growing energy and commitment around the referendum within their own organisations. It was the first real opportunity to connect with supporters. Staff from the three organisations started to go out and present the initiative to their contacts within supportive organisations who could have a multiplier effect.

Using his political contacts, Tiernan connected with the youth wings of all the political parties on campuses across the country.

Two staff, Patrick Sweeney, who had recently joined GLEN directly from DCU where he had graduated in International Relations and Craig Dwyer, targeted the on-campus LGBT societies. They all wanted to be involved and started to collaborate with each other and with the college student unions. By now staff from all three of the organisations were working flat out, contacting their networks and preparing them for the launch.

Meanwhile, a range of merchandise and materials for the campaign was being developed. These included Yes Equality t-shirts, high-visibility vests, YES and TÁ badges, and sweets. Andrew and Tiernan were confident that materials mattered and would be crucial for local events. The steering group agreed nervously to place an order for 10,000 badges. Everyone, Tiernan excepted, wondered how they would get rid of them.

Craig Dwyer had been working on social media and policing and safety issues for GLEN since he had joined the staff in 2013, having completed a Masters in Criminal Justice in Queen's University, Belfast. He now took on the task of handling social media for Register to Vote. He developed Twitter and Facebook designs and Yes Equality website proposals with Diarmuid MacAonghusa from Fusio. Online, people would be asked to check the register on the Department of the Environment website, and if they weren't on it they were to download forms and post them to their local county council. On campus, students would fill out the forms and the student unions would process them and mail them to the relevant county council. Dwyer worked with Fusio to create a 'pledge to vote' Facebook and website app to obtain contact details.

The first post on Yes Equality's Facebook page on 26th September 2014 said that only 30 per cent of eighteen to twenty-five year-olds were registered to vote. It got seven likes. People were asked to invite their friends to like the page, and by 11th October the number had risen to 1,500. The handle @yesequality was not available on Twitter, so the campaign had to settle for @yesequality2015, which went live on 31st October. Craig worked out protocols for posting to ensure that the profile stayed high in Facebook's algorithms.

Tiernan suggested that the launch of Register to Vote should be outside Dublin, and that it should be launched by someone identifiable with, and ideally from, the targeted age-group. It was decided to launch it on Monday 3rd November in Cork and to invite Joanne O'Riordan to do the honours. Joanne was a young, inspiring disability rights campaigner in her first year in University College Cork at the time. She was already well known from media appearances and the film documentary *No Limbs, No Limits*, which she had made with her brother Steven. In her speech Joanne made what would become a key point: 'Younger voters in this referendum have the chance to make a real difference. This voter registration campaign is a critical first step in getting the vote out.'

She was joined in launching the Register to Vote initiative by Eoin Murphy, goalkeeper for All-Ireland hurling champions Kilkenny and education officer of the student union at Waterford Institute of Technology.

While Tiernan, Craig and Andrew were in Cork, Walter Jayawardene managed the media for the launch from Dublin. He, like everyone else, was unsure what response to expect. But they had hit fertile ground both on and offline. The media were looking for new angles on the forthcoming referendum, and this youthful Register to Vote initiative provided one. Most broadcast and print media covered the launch. There was an untapped appetite for information and for ways to participate in the debate, and voter registration fulfilled that. Online commentators could see a new sense of civic responsibility dawning on many, who then became promoters of the message across their social media networks.

The USI and college societies rolled out their on-campus stands. Youth wings of political parties started working on their elected representatives. LGBT organisations ran voter registration events in their community centres.

Craig set up the #registertovote hashtag and analysed tweets and Facebook posts. Across the three weeks the campaign had a six million reach from Irish accounts on Twitter, with nearly

1,900 mentions from 1,000 users.[2] The most shared post was an infographic on how to register which was shared 900 times. The USI hash tag #voterregday was used a further 766 times. The intensity on social media was mirrored by the activity on the campuses. In University College Dublin the Students' Union, political groups and the LGBT society together added 4,000 students to the register. In one day 600 students were registered at the Institute of Technology in Carlow, which represented 10 per cent of the college's student population.

Everyone in GLEN, Marriage Equality and ICCL also reached out to their celebrity contacts. Among those enlisted to support the Register to Vote campaign were movie stars Colin Farrell and Angelica Huston and the comedian and TV presenter Dara Ó Briain. Huston's tweet asking people to register to vote was the most popular of the whole campaign, followed by Ó Briain's tweet 'Whatever your opinion, don't lose your voice' to his 1.85 million followers. Farrell posed with a downloaded poster from the website. The Script and Hozier posed with Register to Vote signs and tweeted support. Yes Equality was particularly delighted when national personalities like the musician Christy Moore, and the Munster Rugby player Duncan Casey pledged their support. Marriage Equality had previously worked with ice-cream manufacturers Ben & Jerry's, who posted a special Facebook banner promoting 'Register to Vote'.

A key early decision by those shaping the campaign was to make all design templates adaptable. The Yes Equality brand was a shared brand. Tiernan and Language were besieged with requests for versions of the Register to Vote logo with the logos of political parties, college societies and civil society organisations. Versions of all the materials were available on the website, including downloadable selfie signs. The executive of the Irish Congress of Trade Unions (ICTU), posed with their branded Register to Vote poster. Moninne worked with SIPTU and other unions to pose with Register to Vote posters at branch meetings. Dale McDermott, chairman of Young Fine Gael, posed with the Taoiseach Enda Kenny. The leaders of every political party posed with the poster. Sinn Féin's national executive posed together. Tánaiste

Joan Burton launched Labour's Register to Vote initiative and linked it in to Yes Equality's. Micheál Martin TD launched the Ógra Fianna Fáil campaign with the shared posters branded with Ógra's logo. Davin Roche worked through the contacts built up through the GLEN Diversity Champions programme to reach out to employers. Among the first groups of employees to pose with the Register to Vote poster were those at Twitter and at Hailo. BeLonG To released a beautifully filmed video, *It's in Your Hands,* which encouraged young people to register. The video was viewed nearly 45,000 times. Greenbow, the LGBT deaf group, made two brilliant videos encouraging deaf people to register to vote. LGBT groups, including local Marriage Equality groups, ran voter registration clinics across the country. Each of these images, films and events was shared on social media, which drove further engagement.

To everyone's surprise, the merchandise ordered in mid-September had begun to run out by early November. The YES and TÁ badges proved particularly popular. Everything had to be reordered. In another of its important early decisions, Yes Equality decided to make Patrick Sweeney its 'Minister for Merchandise'. He assumed responsibility for ordering, distributing and, where possible, commercialising all campaign paraphernalia. The early indicators were that it would prove a mammoth and massively successful task.

The pace heated up as the 25th November closing date for the register drew nearer. More and more well-known names joined the initiative. USI started posting photos of the bundles of registration forms going out to county councils. Urgency was obvious right across social media as people got their friends to check if they were on the register too. Through the combined efforts of Yes Equality, USI, BeLonG To and other partners, the Register to Vote initiative had put at least 40,000 new voters on the electoral register. Register to Vote laid important groundwork, a practice manoeuvre for the referendum campaign that would come.

By 25th November Yes Equality had 20,000 likes on Facebook and nearly 3,500 people had given their contact details, seeking to remain involved in the campaign. The effort had unleashed an energy, enthusiasm and creativity that they had suspected was there but which had not previously found an outlet.

The Yes Equality brand had taken hold. A strategy of establishing a clear design, approach and tone and then letting go of control and empowering others to take their own initiatives had worked. Fledgling groups across the country which had come together for voter registration began to call themselves Yes Equality. The campaign was already going nationwide. The scale of the mobilisation possibilities began to dawn on everyone. A key question was how to move from a voter registration initiative to a referendum campaign.

The success of Register to Vote had made it clear that despite differences in their strategies for achieving marriage equality, the three groups could and must develop a unified campaign if they were to win the referendum. They now began to intensify their focus on the best ways and means of achieving this.

Marriage Equality had developed a 'Road Map to a Referendum Win' as part of a funding drive to donors in late October 2014. This had set out many of the key elements that would appear in the campaign, including canvasser mobilisation, media activity, a bus tour and engagement with strategic partners, such as children's organisations. The task now was to blend with GLEN's and ICCL's plans for the referendum and to identify the staffing, funding and coordination necessary for a winning campaign.

Brian, Gráinne and Mark continued their intensive discussions. They had been strongly advised to recruit a campaign director who had the expertise and experience that were needed. However, there are few such people in Ireland, and none was available. There was also a reluctance by some to bring in external expertise at senior or decision-making levels in a campaign organisation that already had three different groups involved.

They were, however, anxious to tap into those with established political experience who were offering to help out. In November and December Martin Mackin, a former Fianna Fáil general secretary, led round table discussions with the three organisations, and a way of working began to emerge.

On 8th January 2015, in a room in ICCL's building in Blackhall Place, key staff from the three organisations gathered for a special all-day planning session facilitated by Mark Garrett. Mark had been Eamon Gilmore's chief of staff when he was Tánaiste and Labour Party Leader. He was a seasoned hand at political and electoral strategies, and as he reminded everyone at the start of the planning day, he been on the winning and losing side of many a referendum.

The session was a sobering one. The staff and board of the three organisations were probably the best placed in Ireland to know and understand the issue of marriage equality, yet none of them had run a national election or referendum campaign. Mark Garrett was there to alert them to the challenges.

At that time it was expected that the referendum would take place on 8th May and in this planning session, potentially important milestone dates were plotted. It was decided, for example, to aim to launch the campaign thirty days before polling day, since that was the first date on which posters could legally be erected. The advance preparation and the phases of the thirty-day campaign itself were carefully mapped out. It became clear to everyone that the effort would need a small army. Mark pointed out that this would be a much longer campaign than any he had worked with previously; it was likely to run in the media from January to voting day. He warned that one of the greatest dangers of such a long campaign was that it would begin to bore and turn off the middle-ground voters.

At the end of that day, the Yes Equality core team had developed an outline plan, but there was little money, no staff and no campaign.

At this stage, in mid-January 2015, it was decided that because of the inability to find a suitably experienced full-time campaign manager and because of the urgency of the situation, a provisional, integrated campaign structure would be put in place immediately. These provisional arrangements would be reviewed at the beginning of March. Brian and Gráinne agreed to jointly manage the campaign as acting campaign co-directors. Key roles were allotted to staff who volunteered from the three organisations. Meanwhile, volunteers and others from outside the organisations would be invited to act as a campaign advisory group and a communications advisory group. Mark Garrett would chair both. The Steering Group now became the Yes Equality Executive Group, with Kieran Rose from GLEN and Ailbhe Smyth from Marriage Equality joining Gráinne, Brian and Mark Kelly. This group would oversee governance, funding and staffing issues.

The next urgent task was to find an office for the campaign headquarters and to start to move staff and volunteers into it so that that they could begin the actual transformation into the Yes Equality campaign. In mid-January Marie Hamilton, GLEN administration manager, who had been scouring Dublin 1 and 2 for office space, brought the new co-directors to a premises on the first floor of Clarendon House behind the Westbury Hotel in Dublin 2. Gráinne and Brian made a quick decision – the space was small but bright and central. They would make it work. If necessary they would find a larger space later. This rapid decision was to set the pace for many.

Almost immediately Andrew and Moninne from Marriage Equality packed up their offices in Blackhall Place and, along with long-time volunteer Joe Hayes, moved everything over to Clarendon Street. Gráinne began to divide her time between finishing her doctoral thesis and the new Yes Equality office. Brian and the staff from GLEN were finding extra time to work on the Yes Equality campaign. Simon Nugent, who had been special adviser to Pat Rabbitte TD as Minister for Communications, volunteered half-days to the campaign and thereby became its first recruit.

An organogram was drawn up which named roles and people. They established a pattern of 8:30 a.m. meetings three mornings a week. The Yes Equality Executive Group and the two advisory groups began meeting weekly. It took a while for the team to gel. They came from different organisational cultures and had different ways of working. It was clear that it was the collective knowledge, skills and experience, allied to that of the others whom they started to recruit, which were needed to run and win the campaign. Brian and Gráinne led the team meetings jointly. Staff presented draft plans, which were refined and agreed and immediately implemented. There was no time to lose. Brian put a countdown clock on the wall. It didn't seem so bad when it was measured in days; in weeks it was scary. They moved in to the office with 107 days to go.

Events were hotting up around them. On 18th January, Minister for Health Leo Varadkar came out as gay on RTÉ Radio 1. This was an extraordinary moment that ignited the debate on the referendum. On 20th January the first *Claire Byrne Live* show on RTÉ 1 featured a bad-tempered debate on marriage equality that upset many. On TV3 on 12th February Vincent Browne hosted a debate on the referendum which, for an hour and a half, pitched nine speakers in favour of marriage equality against nine opponents. On the same day the Irish Human Rights and Equality Commission became one of the first such bodies in the world to acknowledge marriage as 'a matter of human rights and equality'. The following day, Pat Carey, former Government Minister, came out and was extensively interviewed across the media. On Saturday 14th February there was a turbulent debate on the Claire Byrne radio show on RTÉ, when the Catholic Bishop of Elphin, Kevin Doran, was roundly attacked by Fianna Fáil TD Seán Fleming. The usually mild-mannered Fleming, reared by his widowed mother, took personal offence at Doran's comments on children needing a mother and father in an exchange which presaged the subsequent campaign.

On 20th February the Taoiseach announced that the preferred date for the referendum was 22nd May. The campaign had an extra two weeks.

Money was a critical issue. There was none. Simon set about drafting a campaign budget with fresh eyes and set the figure needed at €300,000. Karen Ciesielski from ICCL and Denise Charlton met and began to identify potential funding routes, including directly asking lesbian and gay people and exploring crowd funding campaigns. Everyone felt sure the funds would come in during the last two or three weeks of the campaign, but they had to commit to expenditure immediately. Brian and Gráinne were confident that the cash would come in eventually. Gráinne was fond of saying, whenever they needed to agree to spend money, 'the two of us will take out credit union loans. We'll be grand!'

The previous autumn a moblisation working group comprising staff of the three organsations had been set up, focusing on the key sectoral and geographical elements of the campaign. As well as Moninne, Tiernan and Andrew, it included Stephen O'Hare and Sandra Irwin Gowran. Stephen, a barrister with ICCL, worked with Gráinne on trying to engage older voters. Sandra examined the geographical challenge with Moninne. Sandra, a former secondary school teacher, was Director of Education Policy at GLEN. It quickly became clear that with Moninne likely to be increasingly absorbed by planning for a Yes Equality bus tour, Sandra was ideally suited to take the lead on nurturing the fledgling Yes Equality groups emerging around the country. This work involved identifying nuclei around which such groups could be built. Some of these were existing LGBT groups, marriage equality groups or just small collections of local activists who wanted to get involved.

Tiernan began intensive engagement with politicians, and with Brian he went to seek the support of the general secretaries of all political parties in linking local councillors, youth wing members and party activists into the emerging Yes Equality groups. Andrew and Walter began the development of the messaging book – the first draft of the answer to every question the campaign could be asked. The public affairs consultant Derek Mooney volunteered to take this first version and shape it into what was called the 'message bible'. Gráinne and Brian started to look for the additional political communications expertise that the campaign needed.

The pace of events was rapidly increasing but there was a vacuum at the centre because there was no formal voice on the Yes side. The No side, whose small pool of advocates was well known, were out in the media and gaining traction. Brian and Gráinne thought that the Yes Equality launch should be brought forward; the Advisory and Yes Equality Executive Groups agreed and 9th March was set for the launch. Intensive preparations began, led by Andrew Hyland, with input from the team and the advisory groups.

The launch was held in the round room of the Rotunda Hospital and was chaired by the former RTÉ news journalist Charlie Bird. He began by introducing Enda Morgan, who told of holding his lesbian daughter in his arms as she sobbed for hours the night she came out to him. It was an experience he wished on no other loving parent he said. He spoke of how he was committed to the Yes Equality campaign because he wanted his daughter Rachel to be able to marry the person she loved. The room fell completely silent as he spoke. The emotion occasionally overcame him but Charlie delicately led him through his story. Enda said he just wanted equality for all four of his children whom he loved equally. 'It's the same love' he said as he described Rachel's love for her partner Marian. He wanted to create an Ireland where no other parent would have to witness a child suffering panic attacks because he or she was gay. He believed that a Yes vote would help to change this for his daughter and for other children.

Charlie then introduced a young lesbian couple, Gill McKenna and Lora Bolger, who wished to be free to marry, and Patrick Dempsey, a young gay man who had been badly bullied in school and wanted a Yes vote to show he could dream like others of getting married and of having his relationship equally recognised in Ireland.

Kieran Rose from GLEN spoke about the forthcoming campaign as 'a great adventure for equality'. He told the gathering: 'As I walked up O'Connell Street this morning, past the GPO where the Proclamation of our democratic republic was declared in 1916 with equality for all citizens as a central principle, I thought it would be a truly fitting celebration of the ideals of the Proclamation if Irish people voted Yes to opening out civil marriage to all its citizens.' Mark Kelly told the launch 'this campaign will be focusing on the truth'. He warned how the No campaign would seek to confuse, but insisted that the campaign would be about having conversations to persuade and convince while not allowing the No side to mislead the electorate.

Gráinne explained that 'Attempts have been made to frame this conversation as if it was about people with family values against the rest of us. Nothing could be further from the truth. We want this referendum to say Yes because we want the freedom to marry because we value family and because we are family ... We are the family values campaign', she proclaimed, deliberately taking ownership of the very territory of family and marriage which the opposition would be expected to claim as theirs.

The launch was extraordinarily well attended; about 300 people turned up, and not just leading figures in the LGBT movement, but people from across civic society and the political parties. It also got extensive coverage both in the mainstream media and online. Not only had Yes Equality announced its existence and asserted its claim as the leading campaigning group on the Yes side, but the launch had also set the tone of measured clarity of purpose. The Yes Equality groups were already emerging all over the country and the campaigns of various partner organisations quickly adopted and replicated this tone and imagery.

With Yes Equality now successfully launched, the leaders of GLEN, Marriage Equality and ICCL turned their minds again to finalising the campaign structure. Mark Garrett and the campaign advisory group put together a detailed memo proposing a series of changes they felt were necessary to ensure the headquarters operation was fit for purpose. Within the Yes Equality Executive Group there were a number of difficult discussions on the most effective structure for the campaign and what external advice and expertise was necessary. After these meetings most of the advisory group proposals were accepted by the executive. The experiment in joint leadership between Brian and Gráinne was not only working, but had turned out to be the best way to bring senior staff from three very different organisations with three different cultures together to run a tight campaign, and the advisory group proposed formalising their roles as co-directors. The Yes Equality Executive agreed.

The two advisory groups were themselves amalgamated and agreed to meet weekly or additionally as needed for the duration of the campaign.

In mid-March Brian had, after the Lawyers for Yes launch, met with Noel Whelan. Noel had done presentations as part of 'How to Win a Referendum' events organised by GLEN the previous September and had then been asked to join the communications advisory group. Noel had been at pains at the group and indeed in his column, to emphasise that the result could not be taken for granted and that the campaign had to focus on the middle-ground. His wife Sinead and others challenged him as to what he was going to do about it and encouraged him to get more involved because it was important. Noel told Brian that with the Easter break in the law term approaching he had some free time that he could volunteer for the campaign. Brian brought the suggestion to the Yes Equality Campaign Executive who liked the idea. Brian, Gráinne and Noel met in Balfes, under the Westbury Hotel, on Monday 23rd March and agreed that his expertise would be of best use to the campaign as a direct adviser to Brian and Gráinne. Noel agreed to start the following day.

There were sixty-one days to go.

CHAPTER 3

I'm Voting Yes,
Ask Me Why

24th MARCH To 7th APRIL 2015

Noel's first day in the Clarendon Street office was Tuesday 24th March. That morning the campaign had taken possession of a second large room in the building. Gráinne and Brian were anxious not to split the growing campaign team, and in particular wanted to ensure that senior staff stayed in touch with everyone else, so they decided to keep the second room for meetings and smaller events.

The three of them spent the day in that second room, sitting down one by one with Tiernan, Sandra, Moninne, Craig and Andrew. It would give Noel a more detailed picture of their functions and a feel for the campaign infrastructure already in place.

In the early afternoon, when they were talking to Tiernan, he told them about something he had seen in the news coverage of the last weekend of the Scottish Independence referendum the previous September. In one report he had spotted a young woman standing on her own in a square in Inverness, wearing a home-made placard on which she had painted the words 'I'm Voting Yes, Ask Me Why'.

'That's it', Noel said. 'That's what we've been looking for.' The others knew what he meant. In their own discussions, and in deliberations with the advisory groups, they had focused increasingly on the need for the Yes campaign to have a soft tone, on the need to defend against a characterisation of it as bullying or threatening, and on the need to tap into the rich vein of personal stories that was already emerging online and offline, which, if communicated authentically to voters, might determine the outcome. They had found the slogan that would capture the spirit of their campaign.

Noel and the other political veterans involved in these discussions had realised that this referendum campaign would have to be very different from its predecessors. To Gráinne, Brian and their colleagues from Marriage Equality and GLEN, this was second nature; from their own work on social causes and LGBT issues they knew that personal stories had a powerful capacity to change minds. The key was to create, in a credible and uncontrived way, a calm environment in which such stories could emerge and be heard. At the same time the campaign had to invite unsure voters to share what was on their minds. It couldn't just claim to be sensitive to the concerns of voters about marriage equality, it had to genuinely engage with their doubts. It would have to reassure them and, above all else, it would have to give voters real stories as a motivation to reach past their apprehensions.

Those simple words, 'I'm Voting Yes, Ask Me Why' captured everything the campaign should be. It was not just a slogan but a strategy. They would tell stories rather than lecture, ask rather than demand, discuss rather than make a political pitch. This moment of clarity informed every other decision during the campaign.

Brian, Gráinne and Noel also spent much time in the next few days revisiting the quantitative and qualitative research, exchanging ideas with people who had worked in previous referendums on social issues in Ireland and talking to some who had worked on the marriage equality campaigns in the United States. It all reassured them that a conversational tone and an emphasis on personal stories was the way to go.

The published opinion polls over the previous year had all shown overwhelming majorities in favour of marriage equality. In recent months two polls had put the Yes vote at about 80 per cent, but everyone in Yes Equality believed that much of this support was very soft and might easily slip away. Poll data, even on a salient issue like marriage equality, is of little value at such a remove from the referendum. Although some politicians, activists and journalists were beginning to take note, the public were still almost entirely disengaged from the issue.

In his presentations to the GLEN events the previous year, Noel had used the analogy of the seating area in a large conference hall to convey how public engagement with the debate develops during a referendum. For a long time before polling day only the first couple of rows are full and then only with political hacks, activists and journalists. It isn't until the campaign properly begins that other rows are filled as people begin to engage, though even then the seating is half-empty. During the last week or ten days the room fills as people begin to tune into the debate and make up their minds.

Yes Equality had already dug deeper. In late January, following detailed Red C polling that examined voting intentions, Peter McDonagh, an adviser on polls for Fianna Fáil, had prepared an analysis for Yes Equality, identifying key target audiences. Arising from this, the research company Bricolage had worked with four carefully tailored focus groups of swing voters. Two of these sessions were with groups of potential Yes voters, one comprising females aged between forty and sixty, the other a mixed male/female group aged twenty-five to thirty-five.

The younger group were thoroughly disengaged from the traditional news agenda and prevailing political discourse. They were, however, intense users of social media, following opinion formers and sharing views online. They were also strongly supportive of marriage equality; many of them wondered why a referendum was even necessary. These younger voters had come of age in a more liberal era. They saw this referendum as being more important than elections. In the words of one young focus group participant, 'It's more about a real issue than voting for people or parties I don't care about...' Although they were passionate and engaged, these twenty-five to thirty-five year-olds were not active. The research report concluded, with some prescience, that 'getting this generation to take ownership of what many saw as their issue would be a key challenge for effecting this change'.

The focus group of middle-aged female voters was more inclusive on the issue than their male counterparts. These women wanted to know and understand the perspective of gay and lesbian people and they accepted a more diverse view of family than that which they felt had been imposed on them. They had little time for church teaching on these or other social issues, but, interestingly, they were often influenced on the topic by their children.

Bricolage also conducted two focus groups with 'soft Yes' voters composed of men between forty and sixty. These were even more revealing. The participants had a sense that the prevailing winds were for Yes and were influenced by political correctness. This partly explained why they said they would vote Yes although they appeared to have no personal connection with the issue. As one of them put it, 'I will vote Yes, but not because I really care either way'. Theirs was a passive 'live and let live' attitude. These middle-aged male soft Yes voters had what the research report termed 'a deep-seated unease about cultural change' and feared that allowing marriage for same-sex couples might reflect a pattern of social change which, as another participant put it, 'might snowball'.

When these middle-aged males were shown media presentations of the No arguments, their inclination towards Yes was disrupted. They were no longer prepared to accept the suggestion that the referendum was just about marriage. The No arguments put to them in the focus groups seemed to confirm existing doubts and they did not understand why the issue of marriage mattered so much to the gay population. This made them susceptible to the suggestion that civil partnership should be enough, and exposed what Bricolage described as 'an urgent need to articulate' why marriage mattered so much to the gay and lesbian community.

Another key recommendation from the research company was that the issue of children and families needed to be addressed head on. The focus groups had confirmed that it was an underlying issue with middle-aged voters of both genders and a particularly significant one for male voters. The Red C poll had confirmed what decades of quantitative and qualitative research had shown: that concerns about children were the soft underbelly of the marriage equality issue. The key question was how to handle the issue in a way with which the majority of the electorate could identify.

The focus groups had shown that the argument for a Yes vote would enable gay and lesbian people to gain full citizenship, it was a powerful trigger. So too were the concepts that marriage is a secure foundation for relationships and a social good, and that gay people are entitled to the same foundation for life together as everybody else. The best response in all groups was to the argument that all children and grandchildren should be able to marry the person they love and that each son or daughter should have the opportunity to celebrate their marriage in the same way as their brothers and sisters, irrespective of their sexual orientation.

The research also gave some useful insights into tactical issues. It showed that having the Iona Institute as the most prominent opponent, at least at this stage, was an advantage for the Yes campaign. Potential swing voters did not warm to Iona's leading spokespersons, who were seen as standing for an 'uptight', 'old world', 'down with that sort of thing', 'reactionary' position which was not attractive to uncertain voters.

The Yes Equality name and branding was also tested, and focus group reaction was moderate. It worked fine, it was not controversial and it suggested the idea of being equal citizens on an unaggressive journey to a shared society.

When the potential impact of various advocates on voters was examined, well-known gay and lesbian personalities received a surprisingly negative response. Instead, these soft voters would best be persuaded by people like themselves, 'someone with a considered view but who may be a surprising Yes'. Mothers and fathers advocating for equality for their own gay and lesbian children worked very well for all groups, as did, unsurprisingly, advocacy from someone like Mary McAleese. Above all else, the research advised using 'opinion formers whom these voters identify with and who are seen to have considered the issue seriously'.

That Friday afternoon at Clarendon Street, Gráinne, Brian and Noel discussed all this research with Vivian Chambers from Bricolage. They particularly focused on the segment of the electorate that would be a recurring topic as the campaign progressed; namely middle-aged males. Males over sixty seemed to be overwhelmingly against marriage equality and appeared immovable. However, it seemed that a majority of men aged between forty and sixty who claimed to be in favour of marriage equality could easily be shifted to vote No, unless the Yes campaign came up with the right message and messengers.

Irish research mirrored that conducted in the United States. Freedom to Marry and the Human Rights Campaign, two groups which had campaigned for marriage equality across the United States had shared their experiences with Yes Equality. In late March Thalia Zepatos, Director of Research and Messaging with Freedom to Marry, visited Dublin and spent a lot of time with Yes Equality's senior staff. Thalia and Freedom to Marry had long associations with Marriage Equality and more recent connections to GLEN.

The American marriage equality movement had learnt its campaign techniques the hard way; they lost twelve State-level popular votes on propositions to ban marriage or to introduce marriage equality before they began to win any. In fact, they had only won their first referendum for marriage equality two years earlier. In many of the unsuccessful campaigns, they had started off with comfortable majorities in the polls, only to see them slip away. Their subsequent research revealed this was because they had run the referendums as traditional LGBT issue campaigns and had focused on mobilising their own base, rather than on engaging with the concerns of middle-ground voters.

Thalia illustrated her key point about the disruptive effect of No campaign messaging by drawing three circles, one inside the other, each representing the layers of a voter's connectivity with the world around them. In the inner circle, which she called 'Me and Mine' is the voter's immediate family. The next is the extended family or neighbourhood with whom they engage less often. The outer circle, which Thalia called 'Others out there', was where everyone else was, in a place remote from each voter's own concerns.

Those who had gay and lesbian people in their immediate family were overwhelmingly in favour of marriage equality, but most people did not share this experience, and to them the concerns of gay and lesbian people were those of 'Others out there'. Polling always showed that most voters were instinctively well disposed to letting gay and lesbian people marry; the initial view was along the lines of 'If it matters to them and has no consequence for me, sure why not?' and 'It's no skin off my nose.' However, marriage equality opponents in referendum campaigns in the United States had always suggested to voters that marriage equality was not just about what 'Others out there' wanted. They had warned that it could have real and frightening consequences for voters and their own families. In this way they persuaded many who initially favoured allowing gay and lesbian people to marry to worry that it could have a downside for their own families and, therefore to vote against it.

Thalia also reiterated some key messages about how the campaign should be presented. Among the things she emphasised was that the right pictures were as important as the right words.

The best strategy for reassuring middle-ground voters was to present gay people and gay couples in the wider context of their families, preferably in group shots where voters had to look closely to guess which of those pictured were lesbian and gay. The research showed that this reminded voters that, like everyone else, gay men and lesbian women had families and communities. The US research also confirmed that older and middle-aged straight couples who after a journey, were expressing support for marriage equality, and parents who insisted on equality for their gay sons and lesbian daughters, were the best advocates with soft voters. Pictures of gay or lesbian couples on their own were out; in research they came across to voters as isolated. 'Why are they always alone?' voters said in focus groups.

The team were also anxious to learn from previous referendums on social issues in Ireland. Around this time the online magazine *Totally Dublin* published a long form article by Jack Gibson under the headline 'How to Win Your Referendum' which focused on the prospects for marriage equality. It included a lengthy interview with Anne Connolly, a prominent liberal activist, who had been a lead campaigner in both the 1986 and the 1995 divorce referendums. Her explanation of why they had lost the first vote but marginally won the second was fascinating.

Connolly told how, between the two divorce referendums, she and others had brought together a diverse group to analyse what had gone wrong, The main thing which emerged, she said, was that voters had a range of different fears which they never got a chance to articulate. 'We had effectively created an environment that shot down these fears, or positioned then as being "Luddite, conservative, reactionary or unsympathetic"… we had been effectively saying "You're uncool if you want to vote No to divorce". The more we created a confrontational, conflictual positioning, the more we were actually pushing them into a No vote mode. We needed to get a deeper understanding of what those fears were about and not just pooh-pooh them.'

Anne Connolly also explained that divorce campaigners had got the tone wrong in 1986. In the second outing, those leading the effort for divorce came together as the Right to Remarry campaign. This time they recognised that the tone '…had to be a lot warmer, more inclusive and understanding, more aimed at the mainstream. We had to position what we were saying,' she stressed. 'You don't necessarily want this [divorce] for yourself – and that's fine, but it is possible to be generous and think of other citizens who want to behave differently. It was then about collecting people who could speak to those fears … theologians across most faiths, journalists and social commentators. And we just facilitated a discussion.'

Reading this in March 2015, those coordinating the Yes Equality campaign saw Connolly's remarks about the change of approach for the 1995 divorce referendum as a succinct summary of what the Yes Equality campaign now also needed to do. If anything, the tone had to be even softer.

The barrister Peter Ward had been a leading spokesperson for Right to Remarry. Now a Senior Counsel, he had also been active, with Mary O'Toole SC, Nick Reilly and GLEN board members Fergus Ryan and Muriel Walls and others in setting up the Lawyers for Yes group for the marriage equality referendum. Brian, Gráinne and Noel decided to ask Peter to join the Yes Equality Advisory Group, where he proved a most useful contributor.

They then had to turn all this analysis into key decisions about strategy and positioning. Using the concept of 'I'm Voting Yes, Ask Me Why', they had to decide what precisely Yes Equality could and should do for the remaining seven weeks and in what order it would be done.

After many discussions, they decided to set their strategic decisions down in a one-page campaign plan. By now the synergy between them was such that Gráinne's first draft was agreed upon instantly by the other two. When they brought it to the Yes Equality Executive Group for approval, Mark Kelly suggested one important amendment, emphasising that the Yes Equality campaign would, if necessary, be robust in countering misleading arguments from the No side.

In its ultimate form, finalised just ten days after the three of them had begun working together, this single page set out the objectives for the remainder of the campaign as being to:

- Lead, support and co-ordinate all the Yes vote activity.
- Orientate the campaign as much as possible towards the middle-ground older audience.
- Reassure, persuade and motivate that target audience to engage with the campaign issue and vote Yes.
- Intensely mobilise core supporters to campaign actively.
- Defend the Yes position, counteract misleading messages and robustly challenge misinformation and fear-mongering.

It was an unequivocal statement that, while of course mobilising their own base, and if necessary rebutting the No arguments, the Yes Equality campaign would be going all out for what they began to call 'the million in the middle'.

The page went on to set out the chronology. There would be three phases to the campaign. The first, which was to run through April to the first week of May, was called 'Starting Conversations'. During these weeks they would encourage people to engage with others in conversations on the issue of marriage equality. Under the banner of 'I'm Voting Yes, Ask me Why', there would be neighbourhood invitation events, larger public gatherings and on-street opportunities for members of the public to speak about why they were voting Yes. The second stage was called 'Full Engagement' and would run from 5th May. It would include a highly visible nationwide canvassing operation, participation in national and local media debates, putting a newsletter through every letter box in the land and a twenty-six-county bus tour. They called the final phase, in the last days of the campaign, 'Closing Argument'. How this would be executed, and what the message would be, was not yet decided. They knew it would involve a massive Get Out the Vote operation, but the rest would depend on what arguments actually worked best, or what No argument most needed final rebuttal.

The one-page plan ended with the following flourish: 'From now on, all our messaging, activity and spending will go to delivering on these objectives and anything else is not our work.'

As well as trying to bring clarity to the objectives and strategy of the campaign, and sorting out the chronology, key decisions were also made to significantly enhance the capacity of campaign HQ.

First and foremost the campaign needed a decision point. There had to be absolute clarity about where the power to make final decisions rested. It couldn't be the Advisory Group or the Yes Equality Executive Group, each of which had useful skill sets, but whose members were best positioned to assist or advise rather than direct. Brian and Gráinne had to be in charge day to day, and while they were advised by Noel and other senior staff, and were open to all inputs, they now assumed *de facto* control.

As the operation grew, it also needed more administrative support and office management. For this task Noel recommended Kathleen Hunt, with whom he had worked on several projects. Kathleen had previously been Operations and Events Manager at Fianna Fáil headquarters. She had since worked on the Mary Davis 2011 presidential election campaign, and more recently for Democracy Matters on their campaign opposing the Seanad Abolition referendum. Kathleen began straight away and assisted by Marie Hamilton, brought a calm efficiency to the office itself and also to the mammoth task of overseeing the design, printing and distribution of mountains of campaign literature. Kathleen's warm and welcoming personality was one of the reasons why the growing team gelled so well. For her part, Kathleen was deeply impressed by the energy of the campaign and by the commitment of the widely diverse group of activists, frequently commenting that any political party would be glad to have them.

There was an urgent need to address an obvious deficit in day-to-day political communications management. As polling day approached, the referendum would attract increasing coverage from the political news and opinion writers. What was needed was a known heavy hitter, someone who could not only pull together the messaging across the various strands, but would have the standing, if not to insist, then at least to persuade the various elements in the wider Yes campaign to take on campaign messages. It needed to be someone whose involvement would in itself illustrate Yes Equality's serious intent to both the political media and the political parties. Ideally, it would be someone the political correspondents and senior editors in the newspapers and broadcasters already knew and trusted.

A consensus developed around recruiting Cathy Madden, who had been deputy Government Press Secretary when Eamon Gilmore was Tánaiste. Arrangements were made to bring her on board. The appointment proved inspired. She quickly established a close working relationship with Andrew, who was generous in welcoming her involvement, and they skilfully marshalled their communications team into a strong media and message management operation. As expected, Cathy gave the campaign additional clout in its efforts to keep senior politicians and prominent activists on message. While Andrew managed the important daily messaging, Cathy led for Yes Equality in the sometimes tense negotiations with media outlets about what and indeed who would be the Yes campaign contribution to their coverage. She engaged on a daily basis with editors, persuading them to use those Yes spokespersons and messengers whom the campaign research and personal instinct told her worked best with the audience for the particular programme and with those elements of the electorate that the campaign most needed to reach. It was also Cathy who would take the heat from those who were displaced and disappointed when editors preferred another spokesperson, even if at times it wasn't her doing.

As well as building on earlier relationships with key media, the campaign set about building closer working relationships with the political parties at the most senior level. Noel and Mark Garrett went to a meeting early one morning to have an initial chat with Alex White TD, who was campaign director for the Labour Party, and the party's then general secretary, David Leech. Labour was going to run a 'full throttle' campaign, seeing it as their own issue; the challenge would be holding their activists back until mid-April when Labour planned to kick off their campaign. They too were conscious that for the campaign to be seen as being government-led would be counter-productive, so they were anxious to work closely with and, if necessary, through Yes Equality. Alex himself was fully committed and, as an experienced politician and a Senior Counsel, was comfortable with the issues surrounding marriage equality. As it happened, he had a brother who was gay, and he was encouraged to tell that story. He would prove to be one of the most effective political performers in the campaign.

The following day Brian, Gráinne and Noel went with Tiernan to meet Simon Coveney TD, the Minister for Agriculture and Defence, who had been appointed Fine Gael's campaign director. Jerry

Buttimer TD, who had been appointed the party's deputy campaign director, was also at the meeting.

They found Coveney focused on his task. He had sought the position of Campaign Director from Taoiseach Enda Kenny, clearly feeling that as a married man and as a non-Dublin Minister in a rural-focused ministry he could play a part in reassuring middle-ground Fine Gael voters. He had a strong and effective narrative on how and why he himself had changed his mind on marriage equality. Coveney was already busily working on reluctant party trustees to get more money for the Fine Gael referendum campaign, and on developing events, posters and literature that targeted the party's key audience.

He was surprised to hear that Yes Equality didn't plan to do posters. 'We don't have the money,' Brian told him. 'We presume the parties are doing them and we are using what funds we have on a bus tour.' Coveney was adamant. 'You have no credibility as a campaign unless you do posters,' he told them; 'even if it means no bus'. He expressed incredulity that Yes Equality didn't have sufficient funds raised.

They took the Minister's point about posters back to the Advisory Group and the Yes Equality Executive who agreed that the money would just have to be found for both a bus tour and a nationwide poster campaign.

Coveney wasn't the only one surprised that the campaign was so weakly funded at that stage. Many who joined the campaign team in the later stages were shocked that substantial funds had not been raised months earlier. However, the reality was that while Marriage Equality had held a series of successful individual fundraising events over the winter and spring, by the end of March there was only €30,000 in the bank. The main problem was that no general fundraising appeal had been made to people with money from mainstream Ireland. This was in part because the rules around campaign finances in Ireland are very strict. Campaigning organisations had to register with the Standards in Public Office Commission. Donations had to be from Irish citizens, while donations were legally capped at €2,500 per person.

Now that Yes Equality was registered and up and running as the lead umbrella organisation for the Yes campaign, they could write asking for donations and go online with crowdfunding initiatives. Both proved surprisingly successful, an indicator of the momentum of the campaign. It required skilled fundraisers and networked people who would be willing to do the asking. The effort was led by Denise Charlton, a board member of Marriage Equality, who took on the task of working with Karen Ciesielski from ICCL to raise the funds needed for the campaign. The task of voluntary senior fundraiser for Yes Equality required all her expertise and persistence. 'I have no pride, give me the names and I will ask them', Denise often used to say. Everyone involved in the campaign was asked repeatedly to produce fundraising leads for Denise and Karen to follow up. Their work was crucial, not least because it enabled the leadership team to get on with their campaign work without having to carry the fundraising burden as well. One lesson learnt early on about fundraising was the value of sending out immediate thank you letters from Brian and Gráinne. Niamh Griffin generated bundles of letters to be personally signed by both that appeared daily on their desk. These 'thank you' notes often led to further donations. The fundraising required close compliance with the requirement of the Standards in Public Office Commission. The identity of all donors over €100 had to be known. Kathleen was a stickler on this point. One man who organised a large dinner party in his house found himself being quizzed by her about the exact home addresses of each of those who had attended.

Having decided to produce posters, Yes Equality now had to decide what they would look like. They sent word to Adam May and his team at Language to come back within five days with ideas. The lead-in time for printing and erecting posters was about two weeks, so, as Kathleen kept reminding everyone, decisions about design would have to be made within the week.

While Language was developing its ideas, other options were being explored. The advertising agency Havas Worldwide offered help through Vivian Chambers of Bricolage. While instinctively loyal to Language, whose designs for Yes Equality were already becoming iconic, the team realised that creative competition would bring added value.

Language pitched four ideas for posters to Brian, Gráinne, Noel, Tiernan, Andrew and Craig on the following Monday afternoon. The first depicted toddlers over a strap line and displayed a message of the importance of being allowed to grow up as equals. This option was quickly dismissed. Using babies on Yes posters for a marriage equality referendum was just not a runner.

The next option showed an older man and woman dressed in Superman and Batman costumes with a tag line which emphasised the superpowers voters had in giving equality. This one brought a smile to all but was parked for later use, perhaps as a second, more light-hearted poster launch.

Adam's third idea was a striking image of Mary McAleese on a poster advocating a Yes vote. Everyone in the room took a deep breath when it was unveiled. It was really arresting, but sadly it was impractical. It might be seen as inappropriate for the former president and was unlikely to be cleared for use by her. It would have been unfair to ask her.

The fourth poster idea from Language was large words on a white background using the now distinctive Yes Equality design and typeface saying, 'Loving, Generous, Equal, Fair, Tolerant' with the strap line 'There are many words to describe Ireland. On 22nd May we just need one – YES.' This concept worked well in large billboard size but it looked as if the words might get cluttered or lost on a smaller poster on a lamp post. There was some debate too about including the word 'Tolerant', which was usually resisted by gay and lesbian campaigners who, understandably, do not see themselves as needing to be tolerated.

The team decided to work up this 'adjectives poster' as a billboard on an ad-mobile for use at a launch the following Friday morning, swapping the word 'Tolerant' for 'Inclusive', but they decided not to go with it for the lamp posts.

They went straight from Adam's presentation to Havas's trendy offices on Leeson Street. There, Bob Coggins, Peter O'Dwyer, Gary

Boylan and their team presented two imaginative concepts that just didn't work. This was due in large part to confusion about the precise brief. It had not been made clear to them that it was for a lamp post poster.

Noel was due to spend the next two weeks in Waterford for court commitments and could only be around the campaign at weekends, and in mid-week would be available solely by email and phone. The group had a clear strategy, a plan for the chronology for the campaign, and they had resolved capacity issues. However, they still did not have a workable poster concept and they were right up against the deadline.

Getting the poster right meant a lot in this campaign. Quite apart from its visual impact, it would be an important statement about message and positioning, and about how the effort for Yes was being led by civil society rather than political parties. It needed to be something striking, something more than the usual mere campaign wallpaper.

Overnight, Havas turned the situation around. They had arrived at a better idea of what was wanted at the meeting and had grasped why the campaign was going with 'I'm Voting Yes, Ask Me Why' as an overall theme. By the next morning they had come up with a poster that captured the essence of the campaign. It showed two speech bubbles – one large one saying Vote Yes, the other giving a short reason why. It could be executed in different striking colours with a slightly different answer on each. It got general approval from those to whom it was circulated for feedback. Gráinne, Brian and Noel decided to execute it in striking red, green and blue versions, with the smaller bubble saying, 'because marriage matters', 'for a fairer Ireland' and 'for a more equal Ireland'.

Before sending it to print, however, they also made sure it would work on a lamp post. At the suggestion of Fianna Fáil's General Secretary, Seán Dorgan, they printed a single copy in full poster size of each of the three and put them up on a pole outside the office on Clarendon Street, so that they could see how they worked *in situ*. When Brian and Gráinne walked out to evaluate their impact on a sunny, warm day in April, they felt that they worked very well. Although the campaign could afford to print and erect only 5,000 of them, the strong design meant they had a disproportionate impact when they went up a week later.

Little did they realise that the No posters, which would go up in the meantime, would be of even greater assistance to the Yes campaign.

CHAPTER 4

Bráinne and their Purpose-Built Political Machine

APRIL–MAY 2015

In Yes campaign headquarters, everybody took to calling them Bráinne. Such was the synergy between Brian and Gráinne as co-directors that their names began to merge. Together they were the axis around which this extraordinary campaign revolved.

By the middle of April, operations at Yes Equality headquarters had settled into a routine that was not to vary much between then and polling day. The weather was good so the office often got very warm when up to thirty people, most of them volunteers, worked in the one space. The number of people also meant that there was a constant struggle to keep workspaces uncluttered. There were regular desk purges with large black bags to remove the detritus. It was usually quiet with most work done by email. Anyone making or taking lengthy or loud phone calls would walk, phone to ear, to find a quiet corridor or cubbyhole elsewhere.

Everyone worked from their own or a hired laptop, connected to the rest of the office and campaign leaders around the country. There were also several WhatsApp groups across the campaign for those co-ordinating different tasks, along with a closed Facebook group where canvassing teams communicated between themselves and with HQ. Everyone involved in the campaign had to get up to speed with the IT systems since they were central to all communications and activities.

Brian and Gráinne sat at a single desk in the centre of the room. There, with increasing confidence, they made the hundreds of big and small decisions necessary to build and steer an increasingly complex political machine.

The desk they shared was parked against another desk in one quarter of the room. The set up in the rest of the room was the same, creating thirty-two workspaces in all. Kathleen Hunt sat next to Gráinne. A regular joke was that, despite the fact that there was a constant depositing of cash on Kathleen's desk as those who had organised fundraising events brought it in, the three shared one printer cord and were often tussling for ownership of it. Tiernan Brady, who spent much of his time out engaging with the political parties and their campaigns, sat next to Kathleen.

Paula Fagan, former Marriage Equality board member and LGBT Helpline Co-ordinator, sat opposite them, overseeing volunteer recruitment and tried to match the skills of the many offering to work full-time on the campaign with the increasingly varied roles which needed to be filled. Lisa Hyland, Andrew's sister, was beside Paula and the two of them, along with Andrew Deering, responded to all those offering to canvass and put them in contact with local groups. Hot seats were located beside Paula and Lisa for volunteers coming in to work on tasks such as fundraising or taking information calls. The occupants often changed a couple of times a day and Brian or Gráinne would often lift their heads to find a new face looking at them.

The corner behind Brian and Gráinne was given over to the communications team, led by Andrew. When Walter decided, like several of the ICCL staff members, to help in Clarendon Street, Andrew and Cathy quickly recognised his skill at building and maintaining relationships with the print and broadcast media and suggested he become part of the Yes Equality communications team. Walter happily obliged and made a considerable contribution to the media effort.

Until the previous March, Jeanne McDonagh had worked as Press Officer with the Bar Council. She then offered to volunteer full-time for the Referendum campaign and, given her experience, immediately became one of Yes Equality's key press personnel. She was given responsibility for updating the talent book of spokespersons, endorsers and people with personal stories, which had been compiled by the campaign and shared as a resource with the media. Because of her law library background, she was also the key conduit to Lawyers for Yes. Jeanne tended to take calls from foreign media and displayed endless patience in dealing with requests for interviews with 'typical' Irish gays. Closer to polling day it became necessary to set up a separate foreign media help desk.

Séamus Dooley, whose job in the real world was as Irish Secretary of the National Union of Journalists, was part of the Advisory Group and was on the board of GLEN. As well as his invaluable media contacts, he had superb writing skills. As a member of the Executive Council of the Irish Congress of Trade Unions and a joint convener of Trade Unionists for Civil Marriage Equality, he operated as an on-site contact to the trade union movement. Séamus also had a sharp political nose, shaped by his years as a newspaper journalist and as former editor of the *Roscommon Champion*. Throughout April he was a regular evening visitor to Clarendon Street, taking up a perch at the communications table. In May he took three weeks' annual leave and volunteered with Yes Equality full-time. He had the ability to reduce the entire office to peals of laughter with his quick wit and commentary – a most useful role in what could be a very stressful space at times. He used to ask repeatedly, for example, that followers should be reminded 'not every thought needs to be tweeted'. Séamus was also the brains behind Hounds for Love, a novel campaign event for Yes supporting dog owners held on Sandymount Strand in May which received extensive media coverage. It even made the lead item on the May Bank Holiday *Six One News* on RTÉ television, contrasting sharply with a stern statement that weekend from the Catholic Archbishop of Armagh.

Both Brian and Gráinne were early starters, arriving at Clarendon Street each morning at about 8.00 a.m. Gráinne was still there most evenings until about 8.00 p.m., when more often than not she went on to speak at a local Yes Equality event or, when she had time, canvassed with her local Yes Equality group. Even when the national campaign got busier, she liked to maintain the canvassing, which gave her a direct feel for what was happening on the ground. Although she and her partner Patricia O'Connor sacrificed most of their personal life during the campaign, Gráinne managed to ground herself by minding their eighteen-month old grandson on Wednesday mornings – a period of sanity she relished when the intensity of the campaign took its toll. Her work on her PhD thesis, on the meaning of civil partnership for same-sex couples in Ireland, had given her useful knowledge that she used in her campaign role. The defence of that thesis also had to be temporarily put aside.

Brian was in the office most nights until at least 10 p.m. and often until well after midnight. Life outside the campaign would just have to wait until after polling day. It was a pattern he had developed over the previous eight hectic but productive years working with GLEN. In Clarendon Street he focused on keeping the increasingly complex and hectic Yes Equality headquarters running smoothly, planning the coming activities and keeping in touch with key advisors and partners. He and Gráinne kept a tight control over, and signed off on all, messaging, campaign materials, videos, press releases and spending decisions, and dealt with the trouble-spots as they arose. This efficiency meant that there was little fire-fighting to do across the campaign.

Each morning there was just time for a coffee and quick chats before the official campaign day started at 8.30 a.m. with morning roll-call, at which each staff member updated their colleagues on their previous day's work. At first these sessions were long and detailed but as the room filled and the campaign revved up, they became shorter, focusing only on major requests or specific information necessary for that day. Reports on political, media and mobilisation campaign developments were quickly made by Tiernan, Andrew, Sandra and Moninne, and then by Davin Roche, on the Businesses for Yes campaign, and by Craig on social media. Walter, Séamus and Cathy each pitched in on media. Everyone who worked in Clarendon Street was invited to sit in on these roll calls and to chip in if they wished. Karen Ciesielski and Suzanne Handley from ICCL also came along most mornings to provide updates on campaign fundraising and financial control.

The communications team had not worked as a group before but quickly developed a bond. Sometimes team members would disappear for a private chat or a break to the Priory Café attached to the nearby Carmelite Church. It was an unlikely venue favoured by Séamus and visiting foreign guests were taken aback to find themselves discussing marriage equality under a statue of St Teresa in the company of Carmelite priests.

They not only generated and organised an increasingly innovative range of events and fielded a steadily rising flow of media queries, but also drove message management and, where necessary, rebuttal. Central to all this was the Briefing Book, an eight-page document which was updated daily and emailed before 9.00 a.m. to a wide list that included all involved in the Yes Equality campaign at national level, co-ordinators at constituency level and those leading the campaigns of partner organisations. In all, it went out to 800 email addresses. Andrew, who at this stage was at his desk each day by 7 a.m., prepared this brief. It was so eagerly awaited that on the few occasions when, usually delayed by Bráinne, he did not get it out on time, there was a deluge of phone calls asking for it. The Book identified key items in each day's newspapers that the campaign had placed and other pieces where the case for Yes was well made. It also pointed to 'must see' coverage of the No campaign and their arguments and gave lines that would counter them. Key messages for that day were succinctly set out. It provided ideas, wording and links for messages to tweet or post on Facebook and flagged events and media outings for the days ahead. This daily Briefing

Book supplemented the larger Message Bible, which detailed Yes Equality arguments on all the important issues. This had already been circulated widely and was updated when required with additional notes on how to respond to new issues as they emerged during the campaign.

Another key part of the communications effort focused on the regional media. Vivienne Clarke, a regional media specialist recommended by Séamus Dooley, had joined the Yes Equality HQ team in early April on a three-day-a-week contract. She had been a former colleague of Gráinne at the *Irish Press* decades earlier. Shortly after her arrival, Vivienne increased her commitment to six days a week on a voluntary basis and thus became another of those whose life was consumed by the campaign. She started by emailing and ringing local newspaper editors and radio producers, introducing the campaign, encouraging coverage and drawing their attention to Yes Equality groups in their area. They were hesitant at first but gradually the local media coverage of the campaign intensified. Indeed, some of the most discriminating and enthusiastic coverage of the campaign happened in the local newspapers and on local radio stations. Opinion pieces from local personalities endorsing the Yes campaign proved to be especially popular with regional editors. In the run-up to polling day virtually every paper carried pieces by diverse personalities, ranging from former ICA president Mamo McDonald to Eurovision winner Charlie McGettigan. A strong opinion piece from Máire Geoghegan-Quinn was also strategically placed in the *Connacht Tribune*.

In the spring of 2015 Yvonne Judge, a senior radio producer with RTÉ, was coming to the end of a two-year sabbatical from her job as editor of the radio station 2FM. Having secured written clearance from RTÉ management that on sabbatical she could participate on the campaign, Yvonne volunteered to work full-time with Yes Equality. She was quickly assigned the task of monitoring broadcast media. For six weeks she spent all her days, and many of her evenings, listening to broadcast debates or items about the referendum on both national and local radio. She used her experience to give immediate assessments of the impact of radio and TV items concerning the referendum, and these were emailed to all the communications and leadership team. Yvonne gave a breakdown of the arguments of each speaker and of the presenter's questioning. She had a replica of an old- fashioned red telephone handset attached to her mobile phone and brought smiles to many faces as she prowled the corridors of Clarendon Street, listening intently with the big red phone gripped to her ear. Her impressive network of contacts, especially across the media and the entertainment industry, proved invaluable to the campaign.

There were others elements to Yes Equality's media monitoring operation. Several of the team had Tweetdeck constantly open on their laptops, as much to monitor breaking news as to keep an eye on Twitter coverage. The campaign's eyes were not just trained on the internet, however. They adopted a 'get your hands black with ink' approach to media monitoring. Several hard copies of the national newspapers, including the tabloids, were purchased for the office each day and once a week a volunteer was sent down to Eason's on O'Connell Street to get a full set of regional newspapers.

When closer assessment of key media events was required, Natalie Lewendon, a volunteer working from home, typed up complete transcripts of debates and programme items. These enabled the campaign to identify usable quotes and to conduct a detailed analysis of what speakers had said, in preparation for later debates. Every word uttered in the media by, for example, Mr Justice Kevin Cross, the Chairman of the Referendum Commission, was transcribed. Much was very useful in rebutting misinformation from the No side. Natalie also transcribed an extended thirty-five-minute presentation by David Quinn, made to an obviously ardent audience, when it was spotted online. It was circulated widely to help campaigners understand the No arguments and narrative.

Each evening at 5.30 p.m. Cathy and Andrew held a half-hour co-ordination meeting with their communications team. If Brian, Gráinne and Noel were around, they sat in. At these meetings the team assessed the day's media, looked at what was likely to be covered that evening or the next morning, reviewed the planning for forthcoming events and updated themselves on the sourcing and placement of opinion pieces and other campaign coverage. These meetings were also central to the updating of a large white board on the office wall which held a calendar of key media events planned by Yes Equality, partner organisations and the political parties. The purpose was to ensure that events across the wider campaign were scheduled carefully so as to avoid media gridlock or diary clashes.

Craig Dwyer also attended these evening meetings of the communications team, making sure that social media was integrated into the overall communications strategy. The foundations of the Yes Equality social media operation, which Craig had put in place at the time of the Register to Vote initiative the previous autumn, were now being built on rapidly. By late April, the marriage referendum was being talked about extensively on both Facebook and Twitter, and Yes Equality's own media operation was playing a key part in fuelling this coverage.

On Twitter, most of this activity was occurring on the #marref hashtag which had actually come into being almost seventeen months earlier. In November 2013 the blogger, disabilities rights campaigner and prolific tweeter, Suzy Byrne, who already had an established reputation as the *de facto* regulator of hashtags for Irish political events, opened a conversation with other tweeters who had covered the Constitutional Convention about what the hashtag for the proposed referendum should be. Among the participants in this decision-making process were William Quill, Ken Curtin and Mark Kelly. They rejected the term #ssmref because, as Kelly put it in a tweet, the 'issue is really that ref won't create "same-sex" marriage, it will open out marriage to all'. Quill added '#ssmref has been shown to emphasise the difference. Talk of marriage emphasises what we all have in common.' Suzy's approach in naming the hashtags for previous referendums had been to create a neutral term that could be used by all sides. She decided it had to be a reporting tag, not a campaigning one, and she knew that terms which had been used up to this point like #marriageequality, were not going to work. Early in the morning of 6th November 2013 she brought the conversation to a halt. 'I need toast to think about it,' she tweeted. Just under an hour later she was back from her toast and had come up with what she felt was the right phrase. At 8.43 a.m. she tweeted, 'Its #marref'. She could never have imagined how many times it would be used. The #marref hashtag became the pivot around which social media discussion of the referendum would revolve. From that moment until the result was declared on 23rd May 2015, more than 890,000 individual tweets would be posted using the #marref hashtag.

As well as making this contribution to coordinating and therefore encouraging the role of Twitter in the campaign, Suzy later made contributions to moderating the tone of the debate. In many ways the starting pistol for the referendum online was the commentary on the marriage equality debate on RTÉ's *Clare Byrne Live* in January 2015. This had not gone well for the proponents of constitutional change. However, tweeters were overwhelmingly in favour of marriage equality and hundreds posted their feelings of exasperation at how the debate had gone. Most had not realised that a Yes in the forthcoming referendum was not a foregone conclusion and that the opponents of marriage equality were well organised, articulate and very good media performers. Many tweeted that disaster loomed. In a piece entitled 'Dear Nervous Ninnies' the next day, Suzy, using her Madame Poulet blog, told people to 'chill the feck out' and accept that some people would vote No and were entitled to do so. 'Implacable courtesy all the way or ignore them' was her advice.

The Yes Equality team were also instrumental in giving the #marref hashtag a renewed profile once the campaign properly began. Its usage spiked again, with 2,860 mentions on 9th March 2015, when Craig used it while livetweeting the Yes Equality launch. It was always apparent that the Twitter demographic overwhelmingly supported the referendum, so it was in Yes Equality's interest that there was a universal standard link that would bring users to all mentions of the campaign.

In addition to Craig, the Yes Equality social media team included Mark Dempsey, Spence Christie and Alan Hatton. They each became highly skilled at finding and posting new material that chimed with Yes Equality's message. Alan, who worked with GLEN, excelled at creating social media graphics with images and quotes from high-profile Yes supporters. Favourable quotes from radio and TV debates which were tweeted or reported in the press, were quickly worked into graphics and everyone involved in the campaign was asked to retweet or repost them. These became a staple of the positive and shareable social media content of the campaign. Useful sound or video clips were posted even before the broadcasters had put them on their own online players. A flood of videos was created by the campaign, by other organisations and by hundreds of individuals explaining why they were supporting a Yes vote. The social media team sifted through all the graphics, artwork, images, and videos to find those which were most effective and then drove their exposure on social media. Brian, Gráinne and Andrew worked closely with Craig and his team to keep the message tight, but the scale of social media engagement became so large, and the volume of content so great that it was almost impossible to keep up with it.

Nor did Yes Equality wish to control all the content. For the national campaign and its local activists, however, it set some clear ground rules. All the social media content generated by the campaign had to be dramatic, exciting and professional looking; it also had to be positive and respectful. From the beginning, headquarters played a part in moderating the tone of the debate and coverage on social media, intervening where it could. At a press conference that took place in late April, the day after the website of pro-life Youth Defence group had been hacked and pro-marriage equality messages placed on it, Gráinne criticised the hackers, saying that those who engaged in such activity were of no assistance to the marriage equality cause. At about the same time many Twitter users began replacing the photos on their accounts with a photo of a prominent No campaigner, Breda O'Brien, overlaid with the Vote Yes twibbon. Yes Equality staff contacted those they knew, asking them to change them back again and once more sent out the word, both online and offline, that this kind of behaviour was counterproductive. While acknowledging the frustration many felt, especially at tweets from some of those opposed to the referendum that were deliberately provocative, Yes Equality encouraged its own activists towards positive messaging.

It was obvious that if the official campaign could be the first responder to news stories and online developments, they could set an upbeat and respectful tone, thereby encouraging others to do the same. They felt that the best way to respond to bad-tempered debates was to feed the growing appetite for news itself, and to raise the profiles of stories that shared their positive messaging. If Yes Equality drove the story, then it would set the tone. Key online contributors were proactively contacted to help ensure this positive approach, and their efforts were mirrored by many other prominent tweeters who quickly spotted what the official campaign was doing.

Many in the established media were also following the discussion about the referendum on Twitter. When, in late April, Brian, Gráinne and Cathy did a series of introductory visits to newspaper editors, they tired of being repeatedly asked about the tone of the debate on social media. Eventually, Brian, in exasperation, asked one editor to point out a single tweet or Facebook message by any Yes Equality group that could be labelled unpleasant in any way. The editor couldn't do so.

Of course the main focus was on the campaign on the ground. The mobilisation team had its own corner of the office in Clarendon Street. There Moninne liaised with the partner organisations while also busily planning and then implementing the bus tour. Working with Moninne on this was Mary McDermott, a long-time feminist activist who volunteered for the campaign early on. At the same table Sandra was kept busy guiding and supporting the Yes Equality groups around the country. Eimear O'Reilly from GLEN and Etain Hobson also became key members of this team.

As the numbers of constituency and local groups grew and the level of canvassing intensified, keeping activists supplied with literature became a bigger challenge. The campaign did its first print run of canvass cards in late February 2015. They were produced in standard DL format on card in full colour and had a variety of executions. Some of them featured well-known personalities calling for a Yes vote. The card with Gay Byrne proved the most popular. Cards featuring the Donegal footballer Eamon McGee and former Tipperary hurling manager Babs Keating also proved popular (except in Kerry and Offaly respectively!). Other popular versions of the canvass card featured Sandra and her partner Marion with Sandra's mother, Maureen Gowran, asking people to support equality for her daughter. Another featured Tiernan's mother, Marie Brady. In all, just over two and a half million literature items were to be printed and distributed by the campaign, including one and a half million canvass cards. In addition to overseeing the merchandising operation, Patrick Sweeney took on the challenge with Sandra of managing the distribution of literature. The campaign initially used a logistics company but with the volume of material involved growing exponentially, Patrick, with Lindsay Puddicombe set up Yes Equality's own distribution centre, hired vans and recruited volunteer drivers.

In early May the campaign also printed an eight-page A4 full-colour newsletter which was distributed to almost every house in the country. It was called *Marriage and Family Matter*. The content was modelled on similar materials used in campaigns in the United States. Parents and families of gay or lesbian people explained how much marriage and family meant to them and how they wanted the same for their children. Clare O'Connell, who had told her story at the Constitutional Convention, and her sister Daire, were pictured with their extended family, while Cork man Conor Cusack was seen with fellow hurlers, speaking of how he should be able to enjoy the same right to marry that they had. The newsletter proved extremely effective. Extra copies were run off for use by canvassing teams. It proved particularly popular at transport hubs.

One of those featured with her family in the newsletter was the TV presenter and producer Anna Nolan, who, with Coco productions, made a number of short films expanding on each of the stories and messages in the newsletter. The campaign arranged a staggered release of these videos on social media to coincide with the arrival of the newsletter into homes.

In another corner of the Clarendon Street office Davin Roche, Director of Workplace Diversity for GLEN, ran a business outreach operation for the Yes Equality campaign. Along with Eimear O'Reilly and Fergal O'Sullivan he prepared and issued thousands of specific Business for Yes posters and stickers for use in workers' canteens, shop fronts or office noticeboards. In Longford alone seventy businesses signed up as Yes Equality supporters. One of the unusual features of this referendum was the extent to which many shops, restaurants and other businesses were prepared to publicly endorse the campaign by putting these stickers in their windows or even by putting up elaborate self-designed Yes Equality window displays. Almost every shop in Finglas village had a poster or sticker in its window, showing the level of positive interaction between canvassers and local business people. It became a memorable feature of the Yes Bus tour that, as soon as the bus arrived, local supporters took the Business for Yes posters and went around local shops getting them put up in shop windows there and then. Fergal, with help from the fundraising team, identified sites and sponsorship for the big Yes Equality wraps and banners that were erected on buildings around the country. Davin and his team also reached out to larger employers, inviting them to publicise their support for marriage equality. Among the first to do this was Twitter, whose Irish Managing Director, Stephen McIntyre, spoke alongside Taoiseach Enda Kenny at a special Tech Leaders Business Case for Marriage event organised by Davin and his team at the Digital Hub in Dublin on the 16th April. The Irish Business and Employers Confederation (IBEC), also came out with a strong statement making the business case for marriage equality.

The warmth of business support in the immediate vicinity of Clarendon Street began to threaten the waistlines of campaign staff. There was a steady flow of complimentary cupcakes, boxes of hand-made chocolates and other confectionaries sent to encourage the team. In an effort to counter this, Brian used to take regular trips to Marks and Spencers to stock up the communal fruit bowls that he insisted were to be put on each set of desks. Discipline on whether or not to eat the wonderful confectionary waxed and waned, though two memorable arrivals resulted in major lapses – a full lunch for thirty people from Saba across the road from the offices, and then a replica of the Yes Bus made by the Cupcake Bloke. Campaign staff spoke about the 'referendum stone' gained.

Every Tuesday morning at 8.00 a.m. the Advisory Group, made up of members of the original communications and strategy groups, met in Clarendon Street. The meetings were chaired by Mark Garrett. Bríd Rosney, one time adviser to President Mary Robinson, was also a member. Other regular attendees included Fergus Finlay, Peter Ward, Martin Mackin, Gary Joyce, Denise Charlton, Senator Katherine Zappone and Séamus Dooley. Mark Kelly for ICCL, Kieran Rose for GLEN and Ailbhe Smyth for Marriage Equality also attended as did Brian, Gráinne and Cathy, as well as Noel, when he was in town. Their primary role was to give strategic direction to the campaign. All key campaign materials, such as posters, literature and videos, were put before them and they advised on the content and tone of responses to issues and arguments as they emerged during the campaign. It had been thought the group might need to meet more often, but with the basic strategy set and seemingly working, and with Brian and Gráinne exerting day-to-day control of the campaign, this did not prove necessary. Most of those attending were also involved in the campaign on a daily basis, and if any real crisis or need for a shift in strategy ever developed, the group could be gathered by conference call.

The Yes Equality Executive Group also met each Tuesday at lunchtime. It acted as a supervisory committee for the overall campaign and for fundraising, financial control, governance and regulatory compliance.

On alternate Wednesday mornings Brian, Gráinne and Tiernan met with senior executive staff of the five main political parties. Tiernan chaired these meetings. It was fascinating for Yes Equality to see these senior party political operatives, who usually engaged in intense political competition with each other, working together for a common cause. Those who attended these meetings included Tom Curran and Vincent Gribbins of Fine Gael, Seán Dorgan and Christabella Feeney of Fianna Fáil, David Leech, Ronan Farren and Brian McDowell of Labour, Dawn Doyle and Joe Lynch of Sinn Féin and Roderic O'Gorman and Chris Green of the Greens. This weekly gathering served as a means of soft coordination between Yes Equality and the political parties and indeed between the political parties themselves. Designed to avoid diary clashes with media events or high-profile canvasses, it allowed Yes Equality to ask the parties to cover some gaps in literature distribution and to exchange details on co-ordinators in each area. Messaging, including the Briefing Book, was also shared, allowing the content and tone to reach down to grass-root level. The general secretaries and others were generous with their time. Each of them was personally committed to the issue. Tom Curran was later to feature prominently in the campaign in another context. At the end of each of these meetings, Brian and Gráinne pressed the party officials on what else the campaign should be doing or should do differently. Their collective response was to suggest that the campaign was going fine; 'steady as she goes' became their mantra.

The political parties had agreed with Yes Equality that although the civil society campaign would begin from early March, it would be better for the parties to hold off starting their public campaigns until the last week in April so that they could be more concentrated and effective. One unfortunate consequence of this was that for a period in mid-April the political correspondents began to criticise the political parties unfairly for their apparent lack of activity in the referendum.

In addition to this liaison with the main political parties, the campaign also had close contact with many of the independents and smaller parties. Several either put in place their own canvassing operation for the referendum or persuaded their core supporters to work with their local Yes Equality group. Opposition politicians made great efforts to discourage voters from using the referendum as an opportunity to express dissatisfaction with the government. The Anti-Austerity Alliance's Paul Murphy TD, for example, made an online video which emphasised the point, while a Socialist Party poster asked voters to hold on to their anger against the government until the next general election with the line '2015 Vote for Equality, 2016 Vote against Austerity'. Ailbhe Smyth linked in for the campaign to People Before Profit, who also strongly advocated a Yes vote while holding their line in opposition to austerity. These and similar interventions by many Independents were important, not least because an intense controversy over the imposition of water charges was raging in the country at the time.

Each Wednesday evening Yes Equality hosted a large gathering with leaders of partner organisations who were running their own campaigns. Seats were set up in a circle in the meeting room for forty or fifty people, one or two from each partner organisation. The capacity and resources of the groups varied greatly but they were all equally committed. Moninne chaired these meetings and when she went on the road with the Yes Bus tour, Gráinne stepped into the role. They followed the format of the daily team meetings, with each group explaining what campaign activity they had been involved in the previous week and what they would do next. Headquarters' personnel told them about their own plans, messaging and events and then invited feedback on the main campaign. The meetings were kept strictly to one hour, and afterwards tea and coffee was provided to give the groups an opportunity to network and exchange ideas.

Central to these meetings and to Yes Equality mobilisation nationally were three groups: Amnesty International, USI and BeLonG To.

Colm O'Gorman attended many of the Wednesday evening meetings at Clarendon Street. In 2007 Amnesty had adopted a global policy calling for an end to discrimination in civil marriage laws and in 2009 their Irish members had voted at their annual conference to actively support a campaign for marriage equality in Ireland. The official launch of the Amnesty referendum campaign took place outside the GPO on the 22nd March. They had expected that a few hundred people would turn up, but in the event 4,000 signed up on Facebook and 3,500 were there on the day. #letsmakehistory was Amnesty's slogan.

Michael Barron, founder of BeLong To, and the director, David Carroll, were regular attenders. He and his colleagues had put together a coalition of fifteen leading children's and youth organisations, including the Children's Rights Alliance, Irish Society for the Prevention of Cruelty to Children (ISPCC), Barnardos and the National Youth Council of Ireland, which came together as part of the BeLonG To Yes campaign. It played a key part in mobilising young people and their families. Many of the organisations that supported the BeLonG To Yes campaign had come a long way in recent years towards supporting marriage equality. BeLonG To published a stunning *Bring Your Family With You* video early on in the campaign. It portrayed efforts by young people to encourage their families to go with them to the polling station. The video featured many leading Irish actors and it got superb traction online. The more colourful elements of the BeLonG To campaign included a mustard-yellow Volkswagen camper van which toured different parts of the country.

Laura Harmon and Annie Hoey of USI also attended these meetings. Laura herself played a significant role in several media outlets advocating for a Yes vote. USI was running a very effective campaign on campuses and online using the slogan #makegráthelaw. The slogan even featured on a striking banner hanging from Dublin's Liberty Hall. USI were also central to a new phase of the voter registration effort.

Once the referendum date had been announced, the Register reopened for another fifteen days before polling day to the 5th of May, during which time unregistered voters, new voters and voters who had moved address could be added to a Supplementary Register entitling them to vote on May 22nd. To do so, however, they had to go through a more rigid registration process, which included having a member of An Garda Síochána stamp and sign the registration form to confirm identity.

The USI and other student unions again put a massive effort into getting students onto this Supplementary Register, along with Yes Equality and the other partner organisations. The directions to those knocking door to door were to follow up with those voters who indicated support by asking if they were registered: some of

'Younger Voters Have A Chance To Make A Real Difference': Joanne O' Riordan and Eoin Murphy with staff and volunteers from GLEN, Marriage Equality and ICCL launch the 'Register To Vote' initiative, 3rd November 2014. (Photo: Sharpix)

Business For Yes: Kieran Rose, Co Chair of GLEN, Taoiseach Enda Kenny TD and Stephen McIntyre, Irish Managing Director of Twitter at 'Tech Leaders Business Case for Marriage Equality' event, 16th April 2015. (Photo: Sharpix)

Standing Up For Your Children: Marie Brady featured on a Yes Equality canvass card seeking equality for her son Tiernan, February 2015.

Standing Up For Your Children: Sandra Irwin-Gowran and her partner Marion featured with Sandra's mother Maureen on a Yes Equality canvass card, February 2015.

Jump For Equality: (L:R) Craig Dwyer, Tiernan Brady, Niamh Griffin, Walter Jayawardene, Andrew Hyland, Sandra Irwin-Gowran, Spence Christie, Patrick Sweeney and Paul Boylan at the launch of Yes Equality's 'adjectives' billboard, 17th April 2015. (Photo: Sharpix)

Marriage Equality is Good for Health: Minister for Health Leo Varadkar TD and Minister of State for Equality Aodhán Ó Ríordáin TD help to launch the campaign for marriage equality by Doctors for Yes and other health workers, April 2015. (Photo: Gareth Chaney/Collins Photos)

The Yes Bus Goes To Wexford: Jessica O'Connor, Philip English, John Ryan, Rebecca Doyle, Colm O' Gorman, Moninne Griffith, Cllr. Anthony Donohoe, and Niamh Griffin pictured during the Yes Bus visit to Gorey, 30th April 2015.

Joan Burton @joanburton · May 18
Lovely to catch up with @YesEquality2015 bus and crew in windswept Limerick. Thanks to local volunteers who joined.
↩   ♺ 20   ★ 19   ...

#isawtheyesbus Tánaiste Joan Burton TD tweets about her meet up with the Yes Bus in Limerick during the campaign, along with Gráinne Healy and Minister for Education Jan O'Sullivan TD.

Because Marriage Matters: Yes Equality's 'speech bubble' posters form a window display at South Great Georges Street in Dublin, May 2015. (Photo: Peter Morrison/AP/PA Images)

Would You Have A Spare TÁ Badge?: Pat Carey poses with the already iconic TÁ badge at the Yes Equality 'TÁ Launch', 6th May 2015. (Photo: Sharpix)

> **"** All of the people who know what they're talking about are telling us that it's absolutely no difference who brings up the children, as love as they're brought up in a loving environment.
>
> **I THINK EVERYONE SHOULD BE EQUAL. I CAN'T SEE WHAT A YES VOTE IS GOING TO DO AGAINST ANYBODY.**
>
> *- Daniel O'Donnell*
>
> **YOUR YES MATTERS ON FRIDAY MAY 22**
>
> **YES EQUALITY.**
>
> #MarRef
> @YesEquality2015

Everyone Should Be Equal: Singer Daniel O'Donnell's support for a Yes vote is quoted in a Yes Equality social media graphic, 15th May 2015.

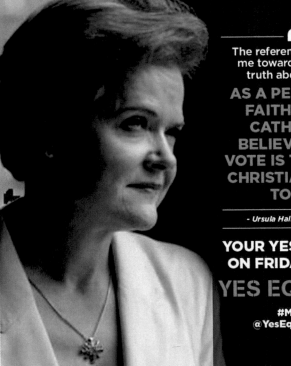

> **"** The referendum pointed me towards telling the truth about myself.
>
> **AS A PERSON OF FAITH AND A CATHOLIC, I BELIEVE A YES VOTE IS THE MOST CHRISTIAN THING TO DO.**
>
> *- Ursula Halligan, journalist*
>
> **YOUR YES MATTERS ON FRIDAY MAY 22**
>
> **YES EQUALITY.**
>
> #MarRef
> @YesEquality2015

Personal Stories: Ursula Halligan quoted in a Yes Equality social media graphic, 15th May 2015. (Photo: Dara Mac Dónaill/ *The Irish Times*)

Even The Dogs On The Street Want Equality: Robyn Neilan and 'Coco' who took part in the Yes Equality's 'Hounds for Love' walk at Sandymount Strand in Dublin, 4th May 2015. (Photo: courtesy Steve Humphries/*Irish Independent*)

Mrs Brown's Address To The Nation: Actress Amy Huberman tweets to promote Brendan O'Carroll's video in support of a Yes vote in the Marriage Equality referendum, 28th April 2015.

Amy Huberman @amyhuberman · Apr 28
Go Mrs.Brown! #YesEquality youtube.com/watch?v=38WRQr

▶ YouTube

Mrs. Brown for Yes Equality

Mrs. Brown for Yes Equality
Mrs. Brown and Lenny Abrahamson join forces for a Yes vote in the Marriage Equality Referendum on May 22nd 2015.

View on web

RETWEETS   FAVORITES
167   224

11:39 AM - 28 Apr 2015 · Details

Lego Equality: Graphics by Debbie Hickey, including this one featuring the Yes Equality Pop-Up Shop at the St Stephen's Green Shopping Centre, were one of the strong visual threads to the Yes campaign. (Photography & Design: Debbie Hickey/ Studio Ten Media)

Campaign Selfie: Mark Kelly from ICCL tweets a picture with Kieran Rose of GLEN and Ailbhe Smith of Marriage Equality after a Yes Equality Executive Group meeting at Yes Equality HQ, 15th May 2015.

 Mark Kelly @Blackhall99 · May 15
In the @YesEquality2015 national distribution centre with @ailbhes and @kieranarose
Amazing work being done!

those most enthusiastic for marriage equality were not. Anecdotal evidence came from various people. Gráinne herself had a discussion at her hairdressers, where all twenty staff were strongly supportive of marriage equality. When she asked each of them individually, she discovered that less than half were actually registered to vote. The combined campaign to get people registered again proved very successful. On the days before the closing date, queues formed at many local council offices as people made the effort to get on the supplementary register, and pictures and publicity about these queues on social media reminded many others to do the same.

One aspect of the registration campaign caused early controversy however. As part of the effort to get people to put themselves on the supplementary register, the campaign decided to do a photo call on Sunday 19th of April. They came up with the idea of having the retired Supreme Court Justice Catherine McGuinness pose on the steps of a city centre Garda station with a Garda and a large mock up of the registration form, in order to emphasise that new voters had to go to a Garda station to register. There was confusion at Yes Equality HQ, however, as to whether the event was being billed as an independent Register to Vote event or a branded Yes Equality event. Brian had approached Pearse Street Garda Station on the basis that it was the former and they had agreed to provide a community Garda on the steps of the station to be part of the photocall.

Unfortunately, the event was not executed as originally intended. Several of those present were wearing Yes Equality T-shirts and many, including Catherine McGuinness, were wearing Yes Equality badges. The media covering the event saw a news angle in the suggestion that it amounted to a politicisation of the police force and it became the main campaign story all that day. When asked about it, the Minister for Justice and several of her colleagues described the Garda involvement as inappropriate and the Garda Commissioner, Nóirín O'Sullivan, herself said that the Garda should not have participated.

There was a tense post-mortem at Yes Equality headquarters the next morning; eventually Gráinne broke the mood, saying, 'Look, no one died. It was an error. It's over, let's move on.' Although it generated immediate media coverage, the controversy got little traction with the public and quickly faded away. If anything, it gave added impetus to the media coverage of the registration campaign. It was a silly early mistake by the campaign and a timely lesson for Yes Equality to avoid over-confidence and be doubly careful in the planning of all their events. Ironically, many people had seen the offending photo in the newspapers and Andrew was receiving congratulatory calls all day from people who spotted the pride-of-place photo but hadn't bothered to read the controversial story underneath. Unfortunately, the controversy fed into a No campaign narrative which claimed that the Yes campaign, supported as it was by the government and all the political parties, was taking liberties, and abandoning the usual protocols and proprieties of campaigning.

Yes Equality were concerned that the incident would affect the reception given to an editorial in the Garda Representative Association magazine, the *Garda Review*, which they had learned would call for a Yes vote. They had seen this as a very exciting development, coming as it did so early in the campaign and from such an unexpected source, and which was likely to have a reach well beyond the 12,000 or so members of the GRA. However, when it was published, it still had a significantly positive impact. The team at Yes Equality were conscious that the tone and strength of the editorial reflected the important work done since G-Force, an organisation for gay and lesbian members of An Garda Síochána had been founded nine years earlier. Its language showed how far many in An Garda Síochána and in society generally had come. The editorial was very strong in its support, saying:

> We have long campaigned for equality for issues of disability, race, gender and sexual orientation within our organisation. The marriage equality referendum is the first time that many of our members will have the opportunity to directly support such equality in the legislative process. Your vote is your voice; together we can make a positive difference.

Dr Richard O'Leary of Faith In Marriage Equality (FIME) attended all the Wednesday evening meetings. This group had been set up by individuals from various religions to show that people of faith could support the referendum. They wanted to act as a counterweight to views put across by conservative Christian organisations such as the Iona Institute. Although a small group, they had a substantial impact among certain audiences. When Church leaders spoke on the referendum, FIME put out press releases independently of the Yes Equality campaign. One of their most innovative ideas was a 'Yesvena' on 20th May (as opposed to a regular Novena) that featured LGBT people of faith such as David Norris and Pat Carey with FIME leaders Brendan Butler, Richard O'Leary, Brian Glennon and the Rev. Stella Jones. In the run up to polling day, they led a tour of important pilgrimage sites around Ireland with Richard O'Leary reporting on the responses they met.

Also present at these meetings were Traolach Ó Buachalla and Emer Nic Dhiarmada of the Irish language branch of Yes Equality. With Andrew they organised a separate special event 'The TÁ launch' which proved to be one of the most evocative moments of the campaign. Pat Carey spoke and traditional musicians played 'Tabhair Dom Do Lámh', the haunting tune which was chosen as the theme of the Tá campaign. Thanks to Traolach and Emer and their colleagues the entire Yes Equality website was translated into Irish and key material, including t-shirts, badges and leaflets, were also made available in Irish.

Trade Unionists for Civil Marriage were usually represented by David Joyce, Equality Officer with the Irish Congress of Trade Unions (ICTU), and by Ethel Buckley, Campaigns and Equality Officer with SIPTU. SIPTU operated a nightly phone bank, with volunteers calling thousands of members to discuss why the union was calling for a Yes vote. IMPACT took out advertising on Dublin buses. Several unions held information meetings. Newly appointed General Secretary of ICTU, Patricia King, led by example, even canvassing fellow members of her local church choir. Smaller groups supported by Yes Equality who assiduously attended these meetings included Doctors for Yes and Librarians for Yes.

Groups who had independently set up online elements of the Yes campaign were also included in these meetings. Among these was Finian Murphy, who developed the Straight Up For Equality site, which involved straight people creating and posting videos saying why they were voting Yes. Finian updated the meetings weekly on the growing number of videos posted. By the end of the campaign more than 10,000 people had posted videos on the website.

Those who visited Clarendon Street each week also included Donal Mulligan, Eoin Wilson and Ewan Kelly, who were behind the #VoteWithUs online initiative in which voters shared their reason for supporting marriage equality. Among the videos which went viral was one by Paddy and Bridget, grandparents and devout Catholics from County Louth, who told of how they wanted 'other couples gay or straight to be able to legally avail of civil marriage and experience the protections and companionship' that they experienced.

From mid-April the Dublin canvass team leaders met as a group at Clarendon Street every Sunday evening. Noel chaired these meetings, which enabled head office to get a stronger feel for what issues were coming up on the doorsteps and what lines the canvassers had found most useful in response. At these gatherings team leaders were also expected to provide detailed summaries of their canvass returns. They showed that across all areas, irrespective of social class and traditional political patterns, there was strong support for a Yes vote in the capital. It was also an opportunity to assess what ground had been covered, to distribute literature and to make sure everyone understood the current messages.

The Dublin groups could also share information and ideas. At one early meeting Yes Equality Dublin Bay South, had an abundance of canvassers and had nearly completed its first round canvass of the constituency, was paired with Yes Equality Dublin Mid-West, which at that stage was chronically short of volunteers.

Because so many of the Dublin canvass teams had been on the doorsteps since early April, they were well positioned to track shifts in support patterns as the campaign progressed. It was at these meetings that the campaign first got a sense of the strong support in working-class areas for the referendum and a determination in those areas to turn out to vote. By the start of May they all spoke of a hardening of attitudes among voters. During early canvassing most voters, whether supporting Yes or No, would politely take or decline literature. Now, the Yes voters were more emphatic, saying things like, 'Oh, we're voting Yes' or 'There are four definite Yes votes in this house.' No voters had also become more emphatic, and were more inclined to give a reason for their vote. In Dublin at least, canvassers thought that this did not represent a shift to the No camp, but rather that No voters were more confident about putting words on the reasons for their vote. There was no evidence at any stage of the supposedly huge silent No vote that was being touted by opponents and discussed in the media.

From mid-April Yes Equality monitored canvassing feedback more closely, not only for the Dublin groups but also for those in the rest of the country. Every night, canvass leaders in all constituencies were sent a text looking for a summary of reactions on the doorstep that evening and an estimate of support levels. The next day they were asked to put more detailed figures and commentary into a shared Google doc. A three-man team of Simon Nugent, Will Peters and Conor King rang around a sample of canvass groups to get more detailed daily feedback.

In the later weeks of the campaign Conor hosted a 10.00 p.m. conference call for Leinster canvass leaders' groups every second night with Brian and Noel. Will hosted a similar call for those in Munster, Connacht and Ulster. These proved useful in monitoring canvass progress, in assessing reaction to media events and in measuring what, if any, issues raised by the No side were arising at the doors, but they were also about boosting morale as energies flagged after six weeks of nightly canvassing.

All these formal ways of monitoring the progress of the campaign were supplemented by a flood of regular texts, emails, and Facebook and WhatsApp messages that everyone in headquarters was getting from their own contacts and informal advisers around the country.

In the last week of April, Brian, Gráinne, Noel and Cathy began daily late conference calls at 10.30 p.m. These lasted for about half an hour and enabled the four of them to use quieter moments away from the office to reflect on the events of the day and focus on overall strategy. As they discussed each day's campaign feedback they soon noted that there was a significant disconnect emerging between the sense of the campaign in the traditional national media and what was happening on social media and on the ground. The traditional media were talking of the Yes campaign being quiet and inactive while they themselves had a sense that something extraordinary was happening throughout the country. Hundreds and hundreds were signing up daily to be part of Yes Equality activity. Something truly magical was taking place at workplaces, in online conversations and on doorsteps. Even by the end of April it was clear that the Yes Equality effort in all its forms was having a real impact. The power of personal stories and the emergence of a massive Yes Equality countrywide canvassing operation was transforming politics.

CHAPTER 5

Tomorrow Will Be Different: Building a Canvassing Army

SEPTEMBER 2014 TO MAY 2015

Over the May 2015 bank holiday weekend Yes Equality published a video that captured the whole nature of the canvass operation. It began with a few lines of scrolling text: 'Throughout history, civil rights' movements have always faced opposition. But with this opposition also comes the opportunity to stand up and make a difference.' Then it segued to Mark O'Mahony, the narrator, his wife, and his young daughter, all canvassers in Dublin South Central. He 'got tired,' he said, 'of listening to the debate, being a spectator', and he wanted to get involved. 'There is a whole world out there', he warned, 'who aren't tuned in to social media. Those are the people we have to reach, people in neighbourhoods all around Ireland who may not be part of the conversation. It's a conversation about fairness.'

The video, which was produced by Peter McGuire and Jean O'Brien, ended with a passionate call for others to get involved. 'I don't want to wake up when all this is said and done and realise that I was one of the generation that said No.' The backing track for the video was a song called 'Home Again', donated by a Dublin band, Delorentos; it had a refrain: 'Tomorrow will be Different', which became one of many anthems of the campaign.

The upsurge in canvassing activity for marriage equality in May 2015 didn't just happen. It was the fruit of much careful discussion, and many months of planning, nurturing and organisational development; initially among the LGBT community and their allies and then more widely.

The planning meetings which ICCL, GLEN and Marriage Equality held during the second half of 2014 had included researching previous social referendums and focusing on turnout. Marriage Equality had previously identified, with the help of a group of referendum anoraks and party experts, the key urban sites where the campaign would require a presence. A strategic decision was made in the autumn of 2014 to focus on these hubs and Andrew, Moninne, Tiernan and Gráinne began to visit existing LGBT groups in these towns to explore how they could evolve into campaign units.

In September 2014 the four of them travelled to the offices of Dundalk Outcomers, a well-established LGBT centre run by Bernadine Quinn. The upstairs resource room in their historic building was laid out with mugs of tea and coffee, cakes and buttered bread. Quinn had invited along members of her own team and allies from the town and surrounding areas who were keen to give their personal support to the embryonic campaign. Over the next two hours the Dundalk team explained what they had done already. Their plans included expanding their area to include Louth, Cavan and Monaghan and they decided they would build a canvass team and a travelling information show so that people at even the most local level could meet and talk to gay and lesbian people and their allies in the lead-up to the poll. The meeting identified what support they needed from the national campaign. On the way back to Dublin, Andrew, Moninne, Tiernan and Gráinne realised that what Dundalk Outcomers had outlined was the model of how a local organisation should work and they set out to ensure that groups in other places could be similarly mobilised.

In October 2014, Yes Equality began holding information and discussion days for partner organisations within the LGBT community. These 'platform meetings' provided opportunities for supporters from LGBT organisations, and later other organisations and individuals to come together to hear plans and take part in discussions about the emerging strategic thinking at national level. They were held in Dublin, usually in The Wood Quay Venue under the Dublin City Council offices, where the original walls of historic Dublin, visible in that space, reminded everyone that the campaign required strong foundations if it was to be successful. The leaders of GLEN, Marriage Equality and ICCL, along with their senior staff, addressed the gatherings, which sometimes included as many as 100 people.[3] Those who attended shared views about strategy and understood what was required at a local level. They also shared views on proposed messaging and structures. The allied activists were relieved to see the three organisations take the lead in putting a national infrastructure in place. Across the country there was a growing confidence that perhaps they could really build a ground campaign that could deliver a Yes majority in the referendum.

At these meetings, Gráinne, Brian and Mark Kelly emphasised how important it was to hit the right tone. Their approach was based on the research which showed that the general demeanour of the campaign and of each of the partners was important. It was explained that the campaign needed people to engage with it and feel welcome. Although it was obvious that some people would like to give the opposition a good thrashing, it was agreed early on that the target group for the campaign efforts was the middle million voters who had not yet made up their minds and who could be persuaded, with the right approach, to become allies, supporters and, most importantly, Yes voters. For many people this involved unwelcome compromise. They were reminded that the best time to respond to those who were already being offensive and trying to draw campaign supporters into abusive online arguments would be to vote yes. People understood that the polls, which the campaign leaders were sharing with them, were stating that a whole swathe of voters were currently unengaged. If the campaign could get the psychology right and move more of them over to 'our side', that would mean a win. Being aggressive with voters would turn them off. The good humour, hope and enthusiasm of these meetings gave those who were to be early canvassers the understanding that while it was important to keep those already convinced on side, time spent head-butting those who could never be persuaded was time wasted. It could be spent more fruitfully convincing and reassuring the moveable middle, which at that early stage looked to be some 40 per cent of the electorate. What was also clear at these meetings was that some supporters were very anxious to get started: indeed, some groups, following their success in the Register to Vote initiative, were already calling themselves Yes Equality. About a dozen of these emerged, many of them in the already identified key geographical areas.

These emerging Yes Equality groups were beginning to make demands of ICCL, GLEN and Marriage Equality. They wanted a national campaign in place, they wanted a plan and they wanted resources to enable them to get out into their local communities and start working.

These platform meetings were taking place at the same time as the *How to Win a Referendum* events which GLEN had designed to dispel complacency or assumptions that the referendum would be easily won.

The week in February 2015 when Yes Equality moved into Clarendon Street was also the week of the very first volunteer training day in the Morrison Hotel. It was organised by Moninne with Ronan Healy of Catapult an event management company and a great supporter of the campaign.

The event kicked off with an uplifting speech by Senator Katherine Zappone and Ann Louise Gilligan. The 300 volunteers in the room were enthralled. Among the groups that had already been established was Yes Equality Donegal, led by Noel Sharkey, who told the meeting that they were determined that even Donegal would say 'Aye' in this referendum. Other fledgling groups spoke of their experiences and how they were gathering members but needed guidance on messaging, campaign materials and canvassing. Senator Averil Power gave an engaging masterclass on canvassing, emphasising that it was infectious and warning people of its addictiveness. Her presentation that day became the template for canvassing training across the country.

Tiernan gave a presentation on the lessons from the Register to Vote initiative, Paula Fagan and Karen Ciesielski of ICCL presented on fundraising, while Andrew, Craig and some staff from Twitter showed the meeting how the campaign might use social media to powerful effect.

On the same day the campaign discovered its most useful canvassing tool when Gráinne, having shared her own personal reasons for being a Yes voter, asked each person there to think of their own and share them briefly with a person they knew beside them. Then, a little more challengingly, everyone in the room was asked to share the same story, now a little honed, with a person they had never met before. The crowd began to buzz quietly and within ten minutes there was a roomful of trainee volunteers with their own personal stories of why they were voting Yes. The Yes Equality army was being equipped to go out and win hearts and minds. Telling stories for visibility and support had long been a successful tactic of the LGBT community. Now their straight allies realised that they too would need to hone their stories and say why a Yes vote was important to them. This gave great relief to those who had been worried about canvassing and were concerned that they would need to be legal experts to hit the doorsteps. With their fears allayed, the volunteers were getting excited and were raring to go home, form groups, get materials from HQ and try it out.

In the hotel lobby Stephen O'Hare from ICCL greeted the participants while other GLEN staff and Marriage Equality volunteers were selling the newly minted t-shirts and handing out leaflets. Dozens of the attendees were also queuing to talk to Sandra who had made a presentation about how local groups could contribute to the campaign. She took the names of those who were offering to be lead co-ordinators in local areas and spent most of the day patiently answering questions, allaying fears and putting people from the same area in contact with one another.

This volunteer day at the Morrison Hotel was the day Yes Equality became flesh. The event had been staged in front of a specially commissioned Yes Equality backdrop and participants heard that campaign materials were in train, that a national office now existed and that it would support and advise their local effort. The Yes Equality army had moved from mere manoeuvres to a war footing.

Volunteers went home that evening feeling that their demands had been met. The staff and leaders were happy that a good start had been made, but they knew that much more needed to be done.

The following week Sandra and Moninne shared and checked contacts in regional areas and identified the gaps. Sandra describes each of the constituency groups as going through phases. Firstly, there was the formation phase. Groups formed, whether through earlier work by Marriage Equality or the Register to Vote initiative, or arising from the volunteer training day. Others began after the office received phone calls from people volunteering to set up a group, or via the dozens of emails that arrived daily. She had to be frank with groups about what support they could expect from HQ and what they were expected to do themselves. Most Yes Equality groups had a mix of LGBT people and straight allies, usually including a sprinkling of party activists who would know the constituency and could teach newcomers about canvassing. Part of Sandra's job was to get the Yes Equality team co-ordinators to sign up to a short protocol document which made it clear to everyone what was expected from local Yes Equality groups and what would be undertaken by headquarters.

An example of one of the early groups was Dublin North Bay. Led by volunteers Ronan Burtenshaw and local independent councillor Cian O'Callaghan. Both of them, had previously been involved in Marriage Equality. They called a meeting on a dark rainy night in February and invited Gráinne along to speak to them. Despite the wet and windy evening, more than forty people turned up in the community centre beside Donnycarney Church. One attendee was Labour Party Minister of State, Aodhán Ó Ríordáin TD. It was clear at the meeting that the elected politicians saw the benefits of allowing a non-party alignment to lead the group. Also at that meeting was Ethel Buckley, Equality Officer with SIPTU; she was there as a local resident. She too pledged support from the floor. It became clear that each of those at the meeting had their own story and wanted to be involved in the campaign. Some were interested in equality arguments, others were parents of lesbian or gay children, and others were lesbian and gay couples who were coming out for the very first time on a political issue. It was agreed that to allow any of the political parties to lead the campaign would be a kiss of death for Yes Equality. This feeling was the same all across the country where similar meetings were held – at times HQ had to intervene to persuade local groups to accept the offers of expertise from local political party members.

Meanwhile, in the same constituency, Senator Averil Power was running a strong canvass team along the coast; Aodhán Ó Ríordáin was canvassing his heartland around Marino and Clontarf; and Ross Golden-Bannon, a board member of Marriage Equality, was leading the effort in Howth, Baldoyle and Sutton. Because the Yes Equality campaign in many areas was a coalition of established groups, this multiplicity of canvass teams in one constituency was not unusual.

In Dublin there were sixteen canvassing teams for twelve constituencies.[4] The largest was that led by John McNamara, Joanna Gilhooley and Justin McAleese in Dublin Bay South. This group had formed in early February when John announced on Facebook that he was interested in organising a Dublin Bay South constituency canvassing team. Over the following fortnight word spread and a group of committed people turned up to the first meeting, which was held in GLEN offices on Exchange Street in Dublin city centre. For John there was 'no rocket science' involved, it was about organisation, discipline and getting the numbers mobilised. The teams went out with twenty to thirty people each evening and over every weekend from March onwards. For their first outing, thirty people canvassed in Sandymount armed with maps of the area and targeted streets. The numbers grew rapidly and ultimately they had about 180 people out nightly. Each of the teams in Dublin Bay South included people whom John described as 'Fianna Fáil grassrooters' who had excellent canvassing knowledge of the area.

John was not a fan of training, so most people who contacted the Dublin South Bay team were told to come along and were allocated to one of the four teams, each of which had a leader with a map. Volunteers were signed into a Whatsapp account and details of where and when they would canvass were posted there every day. The canvass started on time and never waited for latecomers. As the spring weather became warmer, Justin described his sunburnt face as a 'can-tan' acquired by those who were out canvassing for weeks.

Because they had covered their own constituency for the first time by the end of March, Dublin Bay South teams were available to 'adopt' other constituencies. They bused teams to Lucan and Swords and they later led a canvass of Ballymun and Santry. If they said an area would be canvassed, headquarters knew it would happen. Extra leaflets often had to be dropped out to their teams, such was their efficiency. The Dublin Bay South Yes Equality group canvassed an amazing 142,000 houses over the course of the campaign.

Another example of a Yes Equality group in Dublin was that co-ordinated by Darragh Genockey in Dublin South West. This group included many of the local supporters of Senator Katherine Zappone and Ann Louise Gilligan. Darragh's own ambition, at the start of the campaign, was to achieve the highest Yes vote percentage in any constituency. He used a bet with bookmaker Paddy Power as a carrot to motivate himself and his team to do their very best.

Darragh was a former college elections officer at Trinity College Dublin, his sister was a local Labour Party councillor. At its height his team had fifty-six active members, though over the months they had, like other teams, many 'canvass tourists' who came for a night and never returned. Yes Equality Dublin South West started with stands in The Square Shopping Centre in Tallaght and began door-to-door canvassing in mid-February. They found these shopping centre expeditions were great for volunteer recruitment and morale, with lots of passers-by saying 'good on ya'. However, the worry for Darragh and the Dublin West leaders Zappone and Gilligan was how to maintain momentum and how to ensure a big polling day turn-out. They could see the strong Yes support in working-class estates; their concern was how to translate this into actual votes. 'It was 99 per cent perspiration and 1 per cent inspiration,' says Darragh. He liked the clarity that came with decisions from Clarendon Street, such as the suggestion that they hand out the household leaflet the week before the referendum to people getting on the Luas from Tallaght to the city centre. It made sense to give it to people who had time to read it on their journey. Since many newcomers to his team wanted to feel they had been trained to canvass, he led his team through sessions that explained the messages, but he found that once a beginner started canvassing with an experienced person, they got over their fears and had no problem completing return sheets and reporting back to him and to HQ on results. They covered 25,000 homes from the beginning of February to May 22nd.

Meanwhile, Yes Equality Cork, typically, had decided to do things differently and with great creativity. They decided to appoint an experienced political organiser as director for the Cork campaign and chose Ken Curtin, an all-round political expert and then a Fianna Fáil party member. They built canvass teams in all five Cork constituencies, registered separately with the Standards in Public Office Commission, and they set up their own offices on the North Mall. Indeed, Yes Equality Cork had a bigger office space than the Dublin headquarters. Yes Equality Cork was overseen by a strong committee of long-time LGBT activists and seasoned politicos, including Arthur Leahy a board member of GLEN, Dave Roche, Kate Moynihan and Chairman Joe Noonan. While other constituencies ordered their badges from HQ, Cork had their own machine to make badges. They printed some of their own posters and devised canvass materials which, while congruent with

HQ messaging, always had the Cork *blas*! Events were organised throughout the five Cork constituencies. They organised a fundraiser at the Riverside Café in Skibbereen which drew crowds and cash and a similar event in Cobh. Among their more creative initiatives was the recording of 'Song for Equality' by the Choral Con Fusion LGBTS choir in Cork which had its own hashtag #WLTS (We Love The Same). It was heard at many of the Yes Equality events and was another of the theme songs of the campaign. They also arranged a photographic exhibition of very high-quality portraits of some of those involved in the Yes Equality Cork campaign.

It was also Yes Equality Cork who came up with a 'faith letter' handed out outside Catholic churches, which reminded those attending that there were many Catholics who were voting Yes and quoted some of them and their reasons for supporting marriage equality. They got a very positive response, despite traditional political canvassers warning that there was a risk this might be taken as an assault on Catholics.

Over the course of the campaign, Yes Equality Cork attracted more than 800 volunteers. They also delivered 90,000 leaflets to homes across Cork City and suburbs the day before polling. Ken and others on the Cork committee were also in constant contact with Brian to ensure close communication with the national campaign.

One reality that Clarendon Street quickly began to appreciate was the difficulty which many canvassers and LGBT people in particular were facing at some doorsteps. The closed Facebook Yes Equality page had many posts from activists who felt the pressure of putting themselves out publicly when canvassing for a Yes vote. It was hard for LGBT people not to feel the sting of rejection when some members of the public chose to be rude or abusive or even when they were just firm No voters.

A second volunteer day was held in the Communication Workers Union premises on North Circular Road, Dublin on April 11th, and for this Sandra invited psychologist Gerry Hickey along to talk to the volunteers about the need to look after themselves. For the rest of the campaign and for some weeks after, it was something everyone was conscious of. Gerry himself volunteered to run a support service from Outhouse, the LGBT resource centre in Capel Street, Dublin, while another counsellor, Catherine McGee, ran similar one-to-one supports in Galway. Many LGBT people had found telling strangers why they were voting Yes and seeking a positive response in return–at times an extremely painful experience. The campaign co-ordinators were mindful from the outset of the stresses of the canvass and were ready to support and protect anyone who was feeling vulnerable.

Another feature of canvassing of which the campaign leaders became conscious was how disturbing it was for many straight allies in Yes Equality groups when they witnessed the negativity and homophobia experienced by LGBT canvassers at front doors or in public places.

There were some instances at the doorsteps which were more easily absorbed. One canvass crew in a midlands town were followed out of a driveway by a woman sprinkling holy water to 'cleanse her yard' after their visit. In Dublin South Central two young men were warmly welcomed by an elderly lady in Dolphin's Barn who told them repeatedly that she would indeed be voting Yes. 'Of course I'll vote Yes, sure it's not your own fault' was her final word as she wished them well. A definite Yes was welcome, even if expressed in non-PC terms.

Mobilisation and fundraising became two sides of the same coin for the campaign. For example, Dublin Bay South organised a table quiz in Toner's of Baggot Street which was so oversubscribed they had to turn away more than sixty people. They arrived into Clarendon Street the following morning with a list of new volunteers for the campaign and a bag full of coins to be counted and banked. Slattery's of Beggars Bush in Dublin 4, just a few minutes away from the Aviva Stadium, normally flew the flags of competing nations on match days but instead erected eight rainbow flags and allowed collections on the premises, as well as holding fundraising evenings.

Fundraising events had also taken place under the #sharethelove banner organised by Denise Charlton and Paula Fagan before they took up their fundraising and volunteer management roles in Yes

Equality HQ. Speakers at these #sharethelove events included Denise, Gráinne and Colm O'Gorman. The series was launched by Panti Bliss in Pantibar and the events neatly amalgamated both mobilisation and fundraising. Another memorable evening connected to this hashtag was the Zrazy concert, where well-known lesbian jazz duo Maria Walsh and Carole Nelson entertained the crowds at Gotham South restaurant in Stillorgan. It was organised by restaurateur David Barry and his sister Ursula Barry from the School of Social Justice at University College Dublin.

Some fundraising events were more intimate. In Dublin 8, canvassers Melissa Murray and her partner Caroline Butler invited the neighbours to their home, drawing attention to the fact that a referendum on marriage equality was happening and that the outcome was significant for them as a lesbian couple. There were no political speeches, no representatives from Yes Equality, just a series of informal conversations amongst neighbours. As they left, those who attended threw money into a bucket by the door. The event raised €500 for the campaign, but, more importantly, it engaged a neighbourhood in a conversation about the marriage equality referendum.

Other notable Yes Equality events around the country included a 'Fly Your Kite for Marriage Equality' day organised in Tramore, while Yes Equality Cavan-Monaghan had a photo booth in which people could have a photograph taken for a small fee. Cavan also had a 'Big Push' day when a colossal YES on wheels was pushed across the line in the town, raising both funds and awareness.

Hundreds of similar activities across the country generated much-needed early funding. The average donation raised per person was €75. The contribution that these micro- fundraising efforts made to mobilisation was inestimable.

Other events were solely for raising the profile of the referendum and the case for marriage equality. Local Yes Equality groups displayed extraordinary creativity and energy in coming up with new and different event ideas. In Donegal they planted the rainbow flag at the top of their highest peak, Mount Errigal. In Monaghan they canvassed every farmers' market in the county and off-duty postmen plotted routes for the canvassers. In Mullingar they put a gazebo up in the market square every Saturday and talked with all-comers. In Kilkenny they canvassed the main GAA matches and at one game they even teamed up with Yes Equality Tipperary for a joint canvass where their teams were rivals on the pitch. When Senator Ronan Mullen suggested on radio that even if the referendum was popular in Dublin, it might not have the same appeal in somewhere like Clonakilty, Yes Equality Cork and local people had Yes Equality Clonakilty set up in three days, tweeting a picture of them by the entrance sign to the town. In Waterford the local group organised a huge dance flashmob in the city centre. In Sligo they put on a Yes Equality gig at the town's Art Centre. Yes Equality Wicklow produced a series of beautiful photo portraits and videos of well-known local people from all walks of life calling for a Yes vote. In Clare the local Yes Equality group helped organise the launch of #Equalitea events with Pauline McGlynn at the 'Craggy Island Parochial House' of Father Ted fame.

At both national and local level, Yes Equality's attention was constantly focused on innovative ways to attract attention, funds, canvassers and voters.

CHAPTER 6

The Wheels on the Yes Bus Go Round and Round

22nd APRIL TO 22nd MAY 2015

One month before referendum day, on a bright Wednesday morning, a crowd gathered outside City Hall in Dublin to wave off the Yes Bus. Originally Moninne and Gráinne toyed with the idea of asking a celebrity to launch the bus. Instead, they decided that the crowd waving the bus off should be made up primarily of older people: mothers and fathers and grandads and grandmas who were sending the bus off across Ireland, carrying their hopes for a better and kinder future. The idea worked better than they had imagined.

The reasons people turned up for the event were varied and colourful. Among them was Tony Glavin, a grandfather who hoped the bus would help convince people across Ireland that a Yes vote would be a good thing for all grandchildren. Olive Braiden, formerly of the Rape Crisis Centre and former head of The Arts Council, was also there. Madeline Connolly, a woman in her nineties who had thirty-three grandchildren, told Newstalk radio at the launch: 'I'm very disappointed with the Pope. I was sure he was going to be on our side. I'm a Catholic. I go to church.

I know that everyone is going to heaven. … People should vote Yes because God made us all.'

Both Andrew Hyland's parents showed up on that day. Despite his ill-health, his father Andy insisted on being present to show his support and love for his gay son. His mother Eithna spoke candidly to the media. Describing herself as 'not one for campaigning', she said she was there 'for my son'. She was sad that gay people could not get married and was supporting the Yes Equality campaign to support Andrew.

Once the bus hit the road, Andy Wilkinson emerged as an unexpected hero. A burly Scotsman living in Swords, Andy had taken the assignment as a regular driving job. What started as just another job for him soon turned into one of the most exciting experiences of his life. Near the end of the campaign he told Anthea McTeirnan in the *Irish Times* that before he drove the Yes Bus he had met fewer gay people than he could count on one hand. 'Driving the bus teams changed my mind.' Speaking of the fifty men and women who made up the bus teams over the course of the tour, he said, 'They are just normal, loving people and all they want to do is to have the right to live and be happy with the person they love.' Andy got upset at some of the negative experiences suffered by those on the tour. 'I've seen them walking back crying. Anyone who saw that would change their minds. I have,' he said.

The logistics of the bus tour had been put together over many months by Moninne and Mary McDermott. In early April Mary had bargained with the bus companies to get a good price for the month-long rental of the vehicle and the driving team. Before finalising the plans Moninne spoke with those who had run previous political bus tours, such as those put on the road during the Children's Referendum Campaign. She also spoke to Kathleen Hunt and others who had done the same for political parties. All of them warned of how gruelling campaigning on the road could be.

One of the key ambitions of the Yes Bus was to fill the pages of newspapers and the airwaves of radio stations across Ireland with positive stories about the visiting Yes Equality campaign. To achieve this, Moninne worked with Kerry-Ann Conway of Conway Communications and Vivienne Clarke from the communications team at HQ to plan every detail of the media strategy around the bus tour. They settled on a routine of linking up closely with regional papers and local radio stations to let them know when the Yes Bus would be in their area and pointing them to local activists and celebrities who would meet the bus on the day.

On the tour Moninne herself managed relations with those journalists who had been invited to travel. Among them was Kim Bielenberg of the *Irish Independent*, who spent a day with the bus in west Clare. A number of international media members also travelled on board to see first-hand what the campaign was up to. These included crews from the United Kingdom, Germany and France, who spoke to tour volunteers and those who came to meet the bus in an effort to help the international audience for the referendum make sense of the Yes Equality phenomenon.

Each Yes Bus visit to a town had its own flavour. Sometimes it was the local volunteers who had most impact. In Drogheda, Anthony Kinahan from Yes Equality Louth told the crowd, 'I have been with my partner Barry for sixteen years now and we just want to have equal rights.' Sometimes a local celebrity had a special story to tell. The singer and 2005 Eurovision hopeful Joe McCaul came to meet the Yes Bus when it stopped in Athlone. Joe explained how he had come out himself after many years: 'This referendum is very hard for lesbian and gay people, because it's so personal. It's hard putting yourself out there and asking people to vote for your rights, but that's what we've got to do', he said.

When the 2014 *Voice of Ireland* winner Brendan McCahey, a Magheracloone native, joined the Yes Bus in Monaghan he spoke of how, if he had a son and that son was gay, he would like to think he would be 'protecting his son's future' by voting Yes. The comedian Oliver Callan also turned out to meet the bus that day in Monaghan.

Originally, it had been thought that there should be a national celebrity travelling each day on the bus in order to attract local attention. However, it was local people meeting the bus and canvassing from the bus in town squares and shopping centres that really had an impact. One notable exception was the Yes Bus visit to Ballymun when Senator David Norris travelled on it for the day. A huge crowd of local supporters came out to meet him. Also there, waiting to welcome the bus as it rolled into Ballymun, was Pat Carey and local TDs John Lyons and Róisín Shortall. A party atmosphere developed as soon as the doors of the bus opened, helped by the fact that the upbeat Pharell Williams tune 'Happy' was blaring from the Yes Bus's speakers. David charmed everyone, hugging women and kissing children and dogs that were handed to him. The local volunteers in the Ballymun Child and Family Resource Centre baked cakes and hosted a tea party for the bus tour.

The Yes Bus became emblematic. In order to maximise its social media profile and capture the sense of a nationwide tour, volunteers photographed the bus at recognisable locations across Ireland. Among the pictures most retweeted were those of the bus passing Blarney Castle, entering Drogheda through St Lawrence's Gate, and parked on the Mall in Cork. The hashtag #isawtheyesbus became popular on Twitter. People all across the country took to tweeting every time they spotted the bus, thereby plotting its progress. The team often viewed this feed after a long day on the road and it made them smile to see how many people took the trouble to tweet their sighting.

Arrangements were made for the bus to be welcomed at the various trade union centres throughout the country. In Longford, for example, supporters provided a three-course meal in honour of their campaigning guests.

Politicians wanted to be photographed beside the bus everywhere it went. On May 2nd it was in Cork, where Ministers Dara Murphy TD, Simon Coveney TD and Jerry Buttimer TD were pictured with it on Grand Parade, along with the director of Yes Equality Cork Ken Curtin, who was dressed as an elephant or a mouse (he wouldn't confirm which) to welcome the bus to 'the real capital'.

Taoiseach Enda Kenny spent a day on the Yes Bus, starting in Ballina and touring the north-west. The Minister for Justice, Frances

Fitzgerald, met the bus in Clondalkin. Former Tánaiste Eamon Gilmore was warmly welcomed to the bus when, on the last weekend before the poll, a special event with face painting and Yes Equality cupcakes was organised at Dún Laoghaire pier.

The visits made by the bus became occasions for important, and often private, conversations. Mary McDermott recounts how she spoke many times with older women and men who told her poignantly that 'having had the opportunity to marry would have made a big difference to my life'. Many others just wanted to talk or take a selfie with the Yes Bus.

Those who volunteered to campaign on the bus were a varied crew. Some managed their working lives so that they could go out on the Yes Bus for a few days at a time. Others took full weeks off work to go on the road. One volunteer, Karl Ryan, even travelled from Brussels and took the full month off from his job so that he could campaign on the bus all over Ireland. It was exhausting but it was exhilarating. Some days, especially later in the campaign, the crowds were very large but on other occasions, especially in smaller towns, the visit started with just a handful of people who were particularly appreciative that the national campaign had taken the time to visit them. Rain and snow fell during the first day's tour to Louth and Cavan-Monaghan in late April. Cavan town was almost deserted except for the two souls who met the bus as it arrived, but the speakers blared happy music, and as the team leaped out and spread around the town they found people to speak to, or to give badges and sweets or balloons to. The visit changed and conversations about the Yes vote quickly developed. In almost all the places they stopped, local shoppers were delighted to see the colourful bus and its animated crew arrive in their local square or Lidl supermarket car park.

There were also less positive experiences. In Portlaoise, the hometown of Moninne's partner Clodagh Robinson, where they had always been well received as a lesbian couple, a man came over to the bus twice to shout abuse at them. 'People like you should be locked up – like they do in Africa,' he called to the bus team. In Newcastle West a group of men stood outside the bank, leering and jeering at the bus and its occupants. As some townspeople were talking to the bus team, shouts of 'Are you going off with the lezzers and the gay boys?' were heard. A man was so abusive to one of the young men from the bus in Waterford that the gardaí had to be called, while in Dundrum another told Mary that 'This will be the end of humanity if it passes.'

On some visits Mary spotted older women with their husbands who seemed to want to engage, but the men drew the women away from the bus, not wanting to get involved.

The Yes Bus generated a volume of local media coverage worth many times the cost of the tour. The mobilisation of local support and the encouragement for local groups generated was fantastic. The Yes Bus brought the campaign out around the country. Moninne's dream had become a reality.

By the end of the campaign the Yes Bus had travelled 11,000 kilometres over twenty-nine days, stopping at over eighty locations, across all twenty-six counties of the Republic. It more than delivered on its original objectives for the Yes Equality campaign and was a key factor in the win.

CHAPTER 7

The Power of Personal Stories: Some Old, Some New

'I was a good Catholic girl, growing up in 1970s' Ireland where homosexuality was an evil perversion. It was never openly talked about but I knew it was the worst thing on the face of the earth.' Ursula Halligan is political correspondent with Ireland's second national television station, TV3, and one of the most high-profile female journalists in the country. That is how she began a deeply personal and poignant piece in the *Irish Times* on Friday, 16th May 2015. Her decision to tell her story became one of the defining moments of the Yes Equality campaign.

The Yes campaign did not orchestrate the flood of personal stories that shaped the referendum, nor could it. All they hoped to do was to create a calm space in which those who wished to tell of their lives felt welcome to do so and could be heard. For some, availing of the opportunity to be honest about themselves became crucial.

The first inkling Ursula had that she would 'have to do something' during the referendum was in January 2015 when Minister Frances Fitzgerald published the wording of the proposed constitutional amendment. When she read that 'Marriage may be contracted in accordance with law by two persons without distinction as to their sex', Ursula thought, 'Imagine, this might come to pass.' Shortly after this she heard Keith Mills and Paddy Manning, two openly gay men, declare that they would be calling for a No vote. She was horrified at her own silence. At about the same time, as part of her work, she was hearing Fine Gael backbenchers claiming that the marriage referendum 'won't go through'. Her inner turmoil and agitation reached a climax when the arguments about motherhood became part of the No campaign. She felt for all those 'different' families, led by lone parents, or couples, same-sex or otherwise, and knew that she would have to speak out in order to preserve her own sense of integrity.

Before this, the only association in the public mind between her and the issue of marriage equality had arisen from a somewhat surreal event in 2012, when, after the then Tánaiste Eamon Gilmore had described marriage equality as the civil rights issue of our time, she and other journalists pursued the Taoiseach for a response at an event in the National Library in Dublin and he fell over a flowerpot. At the time it led to controversy and a good deal of mockery when his aides complained to the political correspondents' association.

By Easter 2015, which fell in the middle of April, Ursula knew she had to write a piece about herself and her reasons for voting Yes. She began to draft sections on her iPad, sitting at her table at home or on a bench in her garden. She decided at this stage to tell her mother, one of the few people who knew she was lesbian and who had always been very supportive of her daughter, that she was writing the piece. 'Not seeking permission, but wanting her to know' is how she describes this conversation. However, her decision to tell her personal story was overshadowed by a phone call telling her of a dreadful family loss. Her fifty-seven-year-old brother, Aidan, a renowned doctor and deputy chief medical officer for England, had died suddenly.

At the gathering around Aidan's funeral, Ursula spoke to close family for the first time about being a lesbian. The reaction of her family was overwhelmingly supportive. Her other brother, Peter, sent her a quote by Martin Luther King which he reminded her had been one of Aidan's favourite sayings: 'Our lives begin to end the day we become silent about things that matter.'

When she returned to writing the article, Ursula decided to use this quote as the opener. She wrote of the pain and misery of a life held in suspension by fear and disapproval. 'Because of my upbringing, I was revolted at the thought that I was in love with a member of my own sex. This contradiction within me nearly drove me crazy. These two strands of thought jostled within me, pulling in opposite directions'.

Terrified that her secret would become known, she had played the dating game and feigned an interest in men, as so many other gay men and lesbian women have done over the years. This became her life pattern. 'For me there was no first kiss; no engagement party; no wedding. And up until a short time ago, no hope of any of these things', she shared. She saw the writing and publishing of the article as escaping from this silent prison 'completely'.

She approached her friend, the journalist Miriam Lord, who until then was unaware of Ursula's secret and of her decision to come out so publicly. It was Miriam who read the draft piece, agreed to take it to her editor and called Ursula back to say it would be published in the *Irish Times*. The only condition Ursula insisted on was that it would be published in its entirety, unchanged. This was agreed.

Once the article had been prepared for publication, Ursula went into the offices of TV3 to speak to her boss, Andrew Hanlon, the head of news. At first he assumed she was coming in to speak about her recent bereavement and about her schedule for returning to work. Instead, she told him that she would be stepping back from coverage of the referendum because she was publishing an article about being a lesbian, had strong views on the referendum outcome and did not want to have a conflict of interest in her work. His response was entirely supportive and he instantly agreed to reorganise her work schedule. Ursula Halligan walked out of the TV3 offices that day feeling a great weight lift from her shoulders.

The article was posted online early in the morning and went viral immediately. It also took up most of the op-ed page in the print addition. The media coverage of the piece, the number of comments and the outpouring of support and appreciation for this quiet, retiring, private woman's courage was astounding. Here was a deeply spiritual, middle-aged woman with a high public profile telling her story, and it touched tens of thousands of people. She gave older readers, Catholic readers, permission to consider voting Yes. 'As a person of faith and a Catholic, I believe a Yes vote is the most Christian thing to do. I believe the glory of God is the human being, fully alive, and that this includes people who are gay.'

Many people contacted Ursula and the campaign offices to express their thanks to her. Many, many men and women sent flowers and cards saying 'That was my story too that she told.' Her story and its telling on that day moved the hearts and minds of both convinced and unconvinced.

Reading it, those who were gay and had shared their-coming-out-later-in-life experiences were in tears, those who were still in the closet were in awe of her bravery, and those who had escaped the prison of the closet earlier in their own lives were also in tears, because they did not have to endure her life-long experience of feeling 'useless and worthless'. Her plea in the closing paragraph of the article was hugely significant, coming as it did during this last week of the campaign. Ursula said, 'If Ireland votes Yes, it will be about much more than marriage. It will end institutional homophobia. It will say to gay people that they belong, that it's safe to surface and live fully human, loving lives.' She ended the piece by saying, 'Any of them could be your son, daughter, brother, sister, mother, father or best friend. Set them free. Allow them to live full lives.' The searing honesty and obvious authenticity of her message to use the Yes vote as an opportunity to set lesbian and gay people free nudged many uncertain voters towards the Yes side.

For Ursula it was the referendum campaign itself that was life-changing. 'I knew if I was going to tell the truth, I had to tell the whole truth and reveal my backing for a Yes vote', she later said. As a woman who had spent so many decades not telling the full truth about herself, she was mindful of young people reading the article. 'If my story helps even one seventeen-year-old school girl, struggling with her sexuality, it will have been worth it.' It did that and much more. Whatever the outcome, Ursula Halligan was a free woman. Her action was symbolic of the new voices to emerge for LGBT freedom in 2015.

Coming out in public has long been acknowledged as a personal action that can have powerful political consequences. Ursula was a lesbian woman who decided to help the cause of marriage equality during the referendum campaign by telling her story. Eleven years earlier two other women stepped forward, and told of their love and their lives in order to get the issue on the political and legal agenda.

Standing outside the High Court in Dublin in November 2004, after Justice McKechnie had granted them leave to appeal a decision by the Revenue Commissioners which had refused recognition of their Canadian marriage, Katherine Zappone and Ann Louise Gilligan announced to the media that they were seeking recognition for their lifelong loving lesbian relationship. This declaration of same-sex love was revelatory for the Irish public.

'Twenty-three years ago we made a commitment of life partnership to each other' Katherine said, describing their case as 'simply the first steps to seek legal recognition of our lifelong love and faithfulness'. Making the personal political has been a tenet of feminist practice over many decades for those seeking liberation. When Katherine and Ann Louise, two women with public profiles, broke the silence around their lesbian relationship in this dramatic manner, they awoke public awareness to the injustice of the same-sex marriage ban in Ireland. Their public declaration of their love awoke the same possibility in the imagination of the wider Irish public. The fact that these two middle-aged women, feminist theologians, social justice activists and educators, chose to tell their personal business and speak about their love and commitment ignited a wider movement.

Katherine and Ann Louise wanted the right to be married in Ireland, the right to have their Canadian marriage recognised as an equal marriage. This was a right most Irish people took for granted. In December 2006, however, Mrs Justice Dunne found in the High

Court that, under the Irish Constitution, marriage was a right reserved only for a man and a woman.

Speaking that day at the Four Courts, Katherine and Ann Louise, while disappointed at the outcome, said, 'We believe that Ireland will be a land of justice and equality for all human beings. We believe that the Irish Constitution does protect and promote our rights – as it does all others.' They expressed their determination to continue the fight for recognition of their marriage. Speaking later to Mary Wilson on RTÉ radio's *Drivetime* programme, Ann Louise said, 'This judicial decision, its lack of recognition, means that we are not equal in this country in one of the most critical aspects of our lives. You are either equal or you are not. We are not.'

Through their involvement in Marriage Equality over the next decade the two women tenaciously kept to their vision of an Ireland where there would be justice and equality for all. In 2008 they published *Our Lives Out Loud: In Pursuit of Justice and Equality,* which told of their lives together as lesbian women and their battle to get full legal equality for same-sex couples in Ireland. In 2011 Katherine Zappone was nominated to Seanad Éireann.

Their case, their advocacy and their consistent campaigning roused the wider LGBT community, the political system, and many of the Irish public to the possibility of full relationship recognition long before the Yes Equality campaign was even a pipe dream.

There were also many men whose decision to share their personal stories helped to give people reasons to vote yes. The most high-profile of these in the lead in to the referendum was Leo Varadkar, Ireland's young Minister for Health.

At the start of 2015 some in the LGBT community were aware of Leo's intention to come out publicly. When, on January 18th, it was announced that he was to be the guest on the popular morning radio interview programme *Sunday with Miriam,* it seemed that Leo had chosen his moment.

It was Leo's thirty-sixth birthday and the programme began as an occasion for this young, popular Dublin politician to engage in a friendly chat. At first it appeared to be just another easy listening

Sunday morning programme. Then, following a prompt from Miriam O'Callaghan, Leo said it. 'I am a gay man. It's not a secret, but not necessarily something everyone would necessarily know, but it isn't something I've spoken publicly about before.' Immediately Twitter lit up and international news feeds were buzzing with the story that an Irish Minister had declared that he was gay.

Over the course of the hour-long interview Leo spoke warmly of his parents and his sisters, all of whom were supportive of him as the youngest child and baby brother of the family. He spoke of his dad, originally from India and now a retired GP in west Dublin, and of his mother from County Waterford. He described his coming out to them and of their acceptance of him.

He spoke also about his early life as a gay man. He said being gay was 'Not something which defined me'. The demands of politics had consumed most of his life and he had not dwelt on the issue. He told Miriam, however, that with the referendum in the offing, he had decided that the time had come to speak publicly of his sexual identity. He told of how, having agreed to come on the radio programme, he telephoned An Taoiseach Enda Kenny to tell him that he was gay. Enda's response was warm and supportive. The Taoiseach, who had made a high-profile visit to Pantibar the previous Christmas, joked with Leo that he was 'ahead of him' because he had been to the nightclub and Leo hadn't. It was a nice little anecdote, capturing Enda's nonchalant acceptance of the impending announcement by his Health Minister. The Taoiseach told Leo that it was his private life, his private business and none of his concern, and that he would not be commenting on it publicly and he reassured him that 'nothing would change'. No one knew or expected how warm the public reaction to what he had to say would be.

Leo was the most senior Irish politician ever to publicly declare he was gay, and the first serving Cabinet minister to do so. A TD since 2007, his rise within the Fine Gael party had been meteoric and his coming out on national radio was a major boost to those planning the referendum campaign. In truth, it pushed the campaign leadership to agree that an earlier launch date would be necessary, since its effect was to trigger earlier media discussions on what the referendum issues might be.

In the interview, Leo spoke of the forthcoming referendum: 'I'd like the referendum to pass because I'd like to be an equal citizen in my own country. That country [in which] I'm happy to be a member of Government.' He said he did not want people thinking he had any hidden agenda regarding the referendum, which is why he was telling his story now. In thinking about the referendum, Leo said he realised that all his arguments had been dispassionate and detached. He wanted to be able to be passionate about this issue, an issue that affected thousands of others like him who were gay.

The media, both social and mainstream, treated the story of Varadkar's interview as a positive event showing the social progress for LGBT people in Ireland. A Government minister had come out and received an overwhelmingly positive response. Many in the country asked, 'Why not marriage equality now?'

Listening to Leo Varadkar's interview had a particular impact for many gay men. One of those most affected by what the young politician had done was the former Fianna Fáil minister Pat Carey, a sixty-seven-year-old Kerry native now retired from politics.

About a month later, on Thursday 13th February 2015, Pat was doing an interview with Mary Minihan, a political reporter for the *Irish Times*, about Fianna Fáil's preparation for the referendum campaign and he told her that he himself was gay. In a follow-up interview the next day, on RTÉ radio's *Today with Sean O'Rourke*, he explained why he had decided to come out now. 'There are lots of men and indeed women of my generation who have the same difficulty that I had in coming to terms with how you articulate your gender issues,' he said. Referring to Leo's interview a month earlier, he said it had been the catalyst for him to speak out. He knew when he heard it that he 'would speak out if he got a chance'. The approach of the referendum gave him that chance. Losing his role as a TD in the 2011 general election was a 'car crash moment' for him, he told O'Rourke, but it did give him time to reflect on his life and 'to refocus'. He had always been a workaholic, even when he was a primary school teacher in Finglas. He 'never had the confidence or the courage' to speak out about his sexual identity before. 'It gets to a stage where you probably say to yourself, "it's too late for me to start talking about it now". Then he met someone with whom he fell in love, his partner Wai, and he realised that it was never too late.

Pat was born in 1947 and recounted his experiences of growing up in Kerry and then moving to Dublin to become a teacher. The dancehalls in County Kerry were no ballrooms of romance for him as a young man. 'The part of the country I came from, the word gay wasn't even heard of, people were regarded as being "a bit odd", he said. However, even in more recent times, he found that people 'who should know better' would make crude comments about homosexuality; he put this down to a lack of understanding and to some never having been exposed to something that was new for them.

He says his mother knew he was different, although they never spoke openly of his sexuality. 'They wouldn't have had a definition of gay or anything like it. Mothers mightn't articulate it but they always know,' he says. Even when he was in his sixties and a member of Cabinet, he never fully understood his own sexuality: 'I used to say "that person must be gay." It never crossed my mind [that] "I'm one of them". When working in his Ministry for Community, Equality and Gaeltacht Affairs from 2010 to 2011, he was meeting and working with equality groups. 'I never had a light-bulb moment,' he says of his understanding of his sexual identity. He met a man at a social function in 2010 and afterwards he did think they had 'hit it off' and it was 'different'. When he lost his seat and was out of politics he told two of his close political friends, Mary Hanafin, herself a former Minister for Education, whose response was disappointment that he had not told her earlier, and the leader of the party, Micheál Martin TD, who was also supportive of him and wished him well.

Pat, although no longer an elected representative, took the opportunity of his coming out publicly to argue that it would be best if the campaign were led by civic society, such was the negative public attitude towards politicians. 'Maybe political parties should do everybody a great favour and stay out of this debate,' he suggested, 'but realistically there has to be a campaign and political parties are best equipped to organise campaigns.'

Pat's story struck a chord with many Irish people, especially in rural areas. This quietly spoken, gentle man had broken his silence. The response to his public declaration was mostly positive, though a few commentators on social media were still unforgiving of him and his party for what they saw as the financial crisis they had left behind in 2011. Although he no longer held elective office, he attended many public meetings during the referendum campaign, quietly telling his story and explaining why a Yes vote would make such a difference to him. He spoke of those like him who had lived lives of solitude for so long and now had the chance to spend the rest of their lives in a loving relationship, recognised by society and the State. Carey became an unexpected Yes Equality champion.

Another personal story that had an impact early in the campaign was that of Una Mullally. Una was an *Irish Times* columnist, an out lesbian in her early thirties who expressed strong views on many issues, including her support for LGBT rights in general and marriage equality in particular. She had published a book tracing the marriage equality story in Ireland the previous autumn. However, on 27th April 2015, she wrote a column explaining why a Yes vote now had a greater significance for her. She had been diagnosed with cancer.

As it happened, while Pat Carey was coming out on national radio, Una was undergoing tests at St James's Hospital in Dublin. Her stomach had 'been acting weird'. She described in the column how, during the hospital visit, she found herself unable to introduce her partner Sarah as her girlfriend. She was critical of herself, yet her experience was one common to lesbian and gay people in unrecognised relationships who found themselves with a health crisis. A large tumour was discovered in her stomach. She was just five days short of her thirty-second birthday and the diagnosis was obviously shocking for her, her partner, her parents and her friends. It was now also shocking for her readers to hear.

Una wrote of how she had then thrown herself into the referendum campaign; she was canvassing with her local group, Yes Equality Dublin Bay South. She was speaking at public meetings and putting up posters, attending pub quizzes and generally losing herself in the referendum. She said that she could not remain a private person with cancer. She wrote, 'I can't be [silent] during the campaign where LGBT lives are being exposed, dissected, appraised and judged.' Indeed, as a fluent Irish-language speaker she had also participated in referendum debates on the TG4 television station.

Una's story became synonymous with the courage of many LGBT people during the campaign. She concluded her piece with the following plea: 'So here I am. Like any couple, myself and Sarah are not an abstract to be debated on RTÉ. We are real people. These are our real lives. Because when myself and Sarah stand next to our friends, with their boyfriends or girlfriends, or husbands or wives, we know that we are equal. And we are tired of being told that we are not. Our life together is self-evident. We are not lesser than.'

Colm O'Gorman had a high public profile and was not an unexpected champion of marriage equality during the campaign. In his role as Executive Director of Amnesty International in Ireland, he had for many years been pushing that organisation to adopt a pro-marriage equality stance, seeing the issue as one of human rights. Prior to his role with Amnesty, Colm had been a high-profile campaigner for those who had suffered clerical sexual abuse and had himself taken the Catholic Church to court arising from his own abuse at the hands of a Catholic priest, Father Seán Fortune in Wexford. Colm had published a memoir, *Beyond Belief,* and made a documentary, *Suing the Pope,* which recounted this struggle. His work and personal testimony opened the eyes of many Irish people to the extent of the sexual abuse being carried out by members of the Church and the Church's cover up of that abuse. He was one of the most prominent and effective speakers for the Yes side and was passionate in his belief that Ireland had the values of love, inclusiveness and equality at its core. However, he also had a powerful personal story to tell. He had spoken previously, at the Constitutional Convention and elsewhere, of how he and his partner Paul had two adopted children, Safia and Sean, and how theirs was a real and loving family. Indeed, during the campaign, Safia herself spoke on the RTE 1 *Ray D'Arcy Radio Show* about how unfair she felt some of the commentary was about non-traditional families. She spoke beautifully about her loving parents. 'My parents are my parents and I think my family is great, as it happens.' She said 'It should not matter whether a child's parents were a man and a woman or two men or two women as long as the child is loved, cared for and supported.'

Another important feature of the Yes campaign was the willingness of parents of gay and lesbian people to speak out for their children's equality. In March 2015 the former Olympic athlete and now Fine Gael Senator Eamonn Coghlan spoke on *The Marian Finucane Show* about his reaction to his son coming out as gay. He told of his initial confusion about his son's news in a way that struck a chord with many parents in similar circumstances. 'I kept almost blaming myself, asking myself why?' he said. He described his journey to his full acceptance of his son, and from there to a point where he was actively supporting his equality in the referendum campaign.

Another father who went public in support of his son during the campaign was the Fine Gael General Secretary Tom Curran. His surprise piece in the *Irish Independent* on 9th April 2015 had a major impact, not least because his response to his son saying he was gay was one of complete acceptance.

In October 2011 Tom's son, Finnian Curran, was studying for the Leaving Certificate and one evening ran from the house following a row with one of his brothers. He began to run and he kept running through the fields across from their house in rural Meath. He ran until he dropped with exhaustion and, despite calls from his mother and brother, he stayed hidden in the fields for almost three hours. For Finnian, the moment in the maize fields was his epiphany. He later said 'The fact that I was gay had been weighing me down for years and years. I had only told a few of my close friends. Sitting there hidden in the maize, I decided it was just best to get it over with. There was some stress on me at the time, especially with the Leaving Cert. I just needed it out of the way and off my shoulders.'

When he came back to the house, Finnian and his mother sat waiting for Tom to arrive in from work. The three of them then sat in silence for over an hour as Finnian struggled to find the courage to tell his devout parents that he was gay. He feared that they might reject him. They did not. Nor did his siblings when he told them later. 'Sure what does that matter' was the response of one brother and 'So what?' of the other. His sister hugged him and told him she would always be there for him. His family acceptance was complete.

Tom wrote in the piece: 'I am a card-carrying, practising Catholic. I go to Mass every Sunday. I pray every day. I read spiritual books. I reflect and meditate. My life has been shaped by my faith.' He wrote of how as a Donegal man and father of four children, he and his wife Noeleen were originally 'filled with sadness' when Finnian told them he was gay. 'The lovely life she wanted for Finnian, including marriage, seemed to evaporate,' he said. However, Tom could not see how Finnian was any different from his other children. They were each 'carved from the palm of my hand' he said, quoting the words of Isaiah. 'When Finnian told us he was gay, that came back to me, with the deep certainty that I loved him the same as the others, absolutely loved him the same as our other children.'

Tom wrote, 'As a Catholic, seeing his creation as being born out of love, I couldn't see how he was different to my two other sons or my daughter. For me it was fine. I didn't have an issue; I was more concerned about Finnian.'

Since 2011, Tom says, 'I've come on a journey, in terms of my belief and I feel comfortable in urging all people of faith to consider the equal marriage referendum seriously and to vote Yes. In my view, it's the right thing – the moral thing – to do.' For Tom, who had always been a backroom operative, publishing this article was a 'jettisoning' of his privacy. He waived 'the anonymity of a lifetime to publicly affirm my son, and, more importantly, to affirm his equality as a citizen of Ireland and a member of a loving family.'

Tom took the initiative himself, and told nobody in the party in advance what he was doing. He rang Fionnan Sheahan, the editor of the *Irish Independent,* directly, offering the finished article. It was only at that stage that he called his boss, An Taoiseach Enda Kenny, and told him about it. Enda gave his full support and Tom prepared himself for the avalanche of media interest in this extraordinary, yet ordinary story of a man who so loved his son that he was prepared to go public in support of his equality.

Tom had attended the regular meetings that Yes Equality held with senior political party officials. To some he seemed withdrawn at the earlier meetings and when they saw his piece in the *Irish Independent* they realised that he had been considering more than simply how Fine Gael might deliver its referendum strategy.

The referendum campaign required hundreds of gay and lesbian people, their parents, and their adult children to become champions for family diversity. Hundreds wrote letters to newspapers, posted on social media or started conversations about why marriage equality mattered and why all children and parents should be treated equally. Some had been doing it for years, others were inspired, even compelled to do so for the campaign.

Some of those who had been active in GLEN, Marriage Equality and ICCL helped by going very public in the lead up to or during the campaign. Linda Cullen and Feargha Ní Bhroin, both Marriage Equality board members, appeared on the front page of the *Irish Times* the day after polling, pictured voting with their twin daughters Rosa and Tess. This was the most important family outing this family would ever have together. Also pictured in the newspaper that day were Orla Howard and her partner Dr Gráinne Courtney, with one of their daughters, Daire. Moninne and her partner Clodagh appeared in magazines and did interviews for morning TV and radio shows about how marriage equality would mean the world to them and their daughter Edie. They also spoke at numerous public meetings. Not all those public meetings were positive experiences. Moninne recalls an event in her local Church of Ireland church hall a fortnight before the vote. There her family story was greeted with derision and No campaigners shouted at her that she 'should be ashamed of herself' trying to change marriage to include her family.

Sandra Irwin-Gowran, her partner Marion and Sandra's mother, Maureen, sister Paula Murray and her family appeared in national and regional media, making marriage a local issue that mattered to more than just the couple wanting to marry. Paula Fagan and Denise Charlton also put their family out into the media to show the real faces of families who would be affected in a positive way by marriage equality. They did magazine photo shoots in their home and spoke on radio and TV about their desire to be married for themselves and for their two children, Benán and Cian. All around the country, Yes Equality leaders and volunteers went public about being lesbian or gay and explaining why they were voting yes.

Anthony Kinahan and Barry Gardiner from Dundalk had featured in regional and national newspapers, speaking of how they wanted to get married. Having been successful at getting recognised as foster parents, they wanted their civil partnership to be upgraded to full civil marriage and they hoped in the future to be able to be successful in the adoption process. 'We just don't want to feel like second-class citizens any more,' Kinahan said of his civil partnership.

Similarly, Vivian Cummins and Erney Breytenbach from Kildare made videos telling the story of why they wanted their foreign marriage recognised in Ireland and how they had been successfully fostering children for the State for many years. These stories of ordinary people willing to go on the media and be public about their personal lives proved that the personal is indeed political.

In Cork, Margie Fennelly, mother of two gay sons, got involved in the Yes Equality Cork campaign. 'As a mum of two boys who are gay it was a very emotional couple of months,' she says. 'As a parent your natural instinct is to protect your children but so many times during the campaign I didn't feel I could protect them and that just made me feel sick inside. I was so afraid for them and I hated the thought of them hearing the awful stuff being said.' Margie's journey has taken her down unexpected paths. 'I celebrated the day both my sons told us they were gay. It would have been far worse for us all if they could not tell us,' she says. Margie was one of many mothers who went out publicly during the referendum campaign, for her sons and for all the gay sons and daughters of Ireland.

In Offaly, Margaret Gill was another mother who had a real impact. She had been a long-time campaigner for full equality for lesbian and gay people in memory of her daughter Barbara, who had been tragically killed in a road accident, leaving her partner Ruth and their son Stephen in a legal limbo because there was no legal recognition of their relationship possible at the time. During the marriage equality campaign, Margaret spoke often to local and national media. She made a moving and powerful address to the Fianna Fáil Ard Fheis and at various campaign meetings through the country and made a special radio documentary with her husband Bill telling Barbara's story.

Many adult children living in same-sex families or raised by same-sex parents contributed their stories to the campaign. Evan Barry, a film-maker in his mid-twenties, spoke passionately about how he felt as an adult child who had been brought up in a same-sex headed home. There was, he said, 'a lot of talking about me and other kids like me but very little speaking with me.' Evan was involved in the *Voices of Children* research conducted in 2011 for Marriage Equality and also in the making of the short film *Rory's Story*, which depicted the experience of a young man who is refused medical information about his non-biological mother who is gravely ill. During the Yes Equality campaign, Evan and some of his film-making colleagues at Fail Safe films also shot a video, *Every Vote*, urging people to ensure their vote counted. He starred with a number of other adult children in the video, *The Kids Are Alright*, depicting why marriage equality matters to adult children with same-sex parents.

Other stories emerged entirely spontaneously, especially on social media. Anthony Kelly, having seen a No poster saying, 'A Mother's Love is Irreplaceable', posted an emotional piece on Facebook about his own irreplaceable mother. Shortly after she was first diagnosed with a fatal illness, she said to him out of the blue one day, 'I hope that you aren't gay. Your life would be so much easier if you weren't.' He hadn't the courage to answer her. He didn't have to. Just before she died she told him, 'I know. You be whatever you want to be and let nobody stand in your way.' If she was alive now, he says, she would be voting, probably even campaigning, for Yes.

In March 2015 Trinity Students' Union, recognising that most young people were likely to vote Yes, published a terrific online video encouraging young voters to ring their older relatives to have a conversation about marriage equality and ask them to support the referendum. They called it 'Ring Your Granny'. It was a superb example of efforts by the younger generation to actively mobilise and persuade others. One of those inspired by the video was James Mitchell, who then posted his own YouTube clip about what happened when he rang his Nana to have 'the first proper conversation with her ever' about his sexual orientation. He was doing so because he wanted to ask her to vote Yes on May 22nd. 'You don't need to ask me that question,' she said, 'I have been behind you 100 per cent from the day you came out. I have always been your number one fan because you are so brave.' James wept as she told him emphatically that she would be voting Yes. His video went viral.

For the last six weeks of the campaign Yes Equality groups around the country organised special events under the banner 'I'm Voting Yes, Ask Me Why' at which people were invited to speak about their reasons for voting Yes. This series of events was launched on the 9th April at the restaurant of the National Library. Laura Harmon spoke at this event about her own experience of growing up gay in rural Cork. Anne Rigney, a native of Roscommon who had shot to fame online with her impassioned video appeal for a Yes vote, also spoke of how she wanted her son and his partner to have the same right to marry as her daughter. The actress Biddy White Lennon, known to older generations for playing the part of Maggie in *The Riordans*, and Jonathan Irwin, chairman of the charity The Jack and Jill Foundation, each gave moving accounts of how their generation's attitude to gay and lesbian people had evolved over the years. Charlie Bird chaired this first event and then travelled all over the country for similar events in places such as Galway, Ballinasloe, Waterford, Cork and Limerick. The format was simple. There was no top table or podium. After a couple of designated speakers had given their reasons for voting Yes, members of the audience were invited to take the microphone themselves and share their reasons for supporting the referendum. The events were held in hotels, in pubs, in community centres and sometimes on a smaller scale in private homes. This informality created a dynamic which gave rise to an outpouring of personal stories. Many of these accounts were deeply moving and were told in public for the first time. Speakers spoke with passion, with emotion, with regret and, above all, they spoke with hope that the referendum would be carried.

Eimear O'Reilly coordinated these 'I'm Voting Yes, Ask Me Why' events from Clarendon Street with the local groups. Vivienne Clarke chaired one in Hugh Lynch's pub in Offaly on 1st May. Michelle Thomas, who had been media trainer for Marriage Equality for many years, facilitated a packed gathering in Donegal town where once again local politicians and ordinary people stood up to say why they were voting for marriage equality. Séamus Dooley chaired the last meeting in the series in Castlerea in Roscommon.

It was an extraordinary feature of the Yes campaign that all these people and so many others across Ireland were prepared to speak out in local or national media, at local events or to their own social networks, telling why they were voting Yes. It took courage for each of them to go public in such detail about themselves and their families. The bravery and unselfishness of their testimony moved the hearts and minds of many voters.

CHAPTER 8

Posters, Pulpits and Prime Time

17th APRIL TO 17th MAY 2015

The main organisation on the No side of the referendum, Mothers and Fathers Matter, kicked off its campaign with a press conference in the Davenport Hotel in Dublin on Friday 17th April. The setting and staging were impressive and they fielded no fewer than six spokespersons, most of them hitherto unknown. However, the question and answer session became a bit shambolic, when, unable to cite authority for some of their claims, the platform party turned on the assembled media.

From their offices in Clarendon Street, Yes Equality followed the coverage of the launch with great interest, looking for indicators as to what shape the No campaign would take. It had always been expected that new faces would emerge to front the No message in the last weeks. While some of the prominent personalities from the Iona Institute, and David Quinn in particular, were strong media performers, they themselves apparently saw a need to distance the presentation of their case from traditional Catholic conservative causes, or at least to diversify their line-up. Keith Mills, a blogger and Eurovision Song Contest commentator, as well as a gay man opposed to marriage equality, was well suited to their purpose. They also had a selection of young, presentable and articulate spokespersons, some of whom had a medical or legal background.

Yes Equality's assessment was that, with the benefit of the court judgement in the Coughlan case, which required the broadcast media to give balanced coverage to both sides, the No campaigners would run a very strong and carefully coordinated media effort. They also believed that Mothers and Fathers Matter had limited reach. It had very few activists on the ground and was unlikely to have a large footprint on the doorsteps.

It was clear, however, that, as well as tapping into international anti-marriage equality networks and having some very experienced strategists of their own, Mothers and Fathers Matter did not want for money. What they lacked in activism, they would more than make up for with professional postering, literature and a paid for online presence.

In the week beginning 21st April the No side started putting up its posters. As soon as the Yes Equality leaders saw them, they knew that the market research of their opponents had mirrored their own. The No posters went straight for the weak underbelly of public concern, not about same-sex marriage itself but about same-sex parenting. David Quinn and his colleagues had clearly appreciated that if the referendum was fought purely on the question of the entitlement of same-sex couples to marry, they would lose, but if they could turn the focus onto same-sex parenting, then they were in with a chance of defeating the proposal, or could at least contain the size of the Yes victory.

The No posters were a little larger than a standard election poster and were each executed in three colours: red, white and green. They were striking and they were everywhere. The politicos advising the Yes campaign estimated, on the basis of the intensity of the No postering in the capital and their spread throughout the country, that Mothers and Fathers Matter had put up at least 30,000 posters. It was the most extensive postering campaign seen in Ireland outside a general election. At an estimated cost of €10 per poster for materials, printing, erecting, take down and disposal, this suggested a very well-resourced No campaign.

One of the No posters showed a happy man and woman on each side of a smiling baby above the strapline: 'Children Deserve a Mother and a Father'. The central message of the No campaign was that two biological parents of opposite sex are the ideal form of family, that same-sex marriage somehow endangers that and, by implication, that other forms of family are less deserving.

Almost immediately there was a strong backlash to this poster, some of it from sectors of society who, while broadly supportive, had remained somewhat disengaged from the campaign. The posters not only annoyed thousands of same-sex households but also angered hundreds of thousands of people reared or rearing children in households headed by lone parents. On that Wednesday, for example, Yes Equality Dublin Bay South were out canvassing in the inner city and texted the people in Clarendon Street to say they were getting a very strong reaction against this poster in particular.

The Yes campaign's response to this sort of message had been carefully designed well before the referendum. Spokespersons were encouraged to speak of how most children in Ireland are reared by two biological parents and how that would continue to be the situation after the referendum, irrespective of the outcome, but that many other children are reared, and reared equally well, in different types of households. The message that speakers were encouraged to get across was that quality of parenting in our complicated world is determined by caring skills and capacity for love and not by the number, gender, age or sexual orientation of parents. Yes Equality also regularly rebutted the suggestion from the No campaign, that, all else being equal, it is better for a child to be reared by its natural father and mother. A number of presenters on radio shows had taken to repeating this line in questioning. Yes spokespersons were encouraged to dismiss this question as not reflecting reality and as being an insult to other forms of households. The best response was along the lines of 'Each and every family situation is distinct. Our laws and our Constitution should support and recognise these different realities and do so equally.'

Another key part of the counter-argument which Yes Equality encouraged spokespersons and supporters to emphasise was that frontline children's and youth organisations were in favour of and indeed campaigning for marriage equality. Canvassers quickly found that pointing out that organisations such as Barnardos and the Irish Society for the Prevention of Cruelty to Children (ISPCC) supported the referendum worked well on the doorsteps. Another effective response from the Yes Equality campaign was to have adult children of gay and lesbian couples tell of their upbringing.

The second No poster had the word 'Surrogacy' in bold capitals above a picture of a toddler girl and the slogan 'She Needs Her Mother For Life, Not Just for Nine Months'. Yes Equality had expected that surrogacy would be used by No campaigners as an issue in the campaign but were surprised to see it done so soon and so starkly.

It was a difficult issue to counter. No advocates brought it up early in most media outings and then dwelt on the detail of what surrogacy involved. This was discomforting for many viewers and listeners who were hearing about surrogacy for the first time. No speakers usually then went on to link surrogacy with gay parenting. While many in the Yes campaign shared general public concerns about commercial surrogacy, the campaign resented and resisted the suggestion that it was relevant to the marriage equality referendum. The fact that surrogacy was still unregulated fed into some of these fears, although the No side was likely to have made it an issue in any case.

It took a while for the Yes campaign to break through in response to the issue of surrogacy. It came to dominate some of the media events and was frequently raised on doorsteps. The response which eventually got traction was to point out that very few surrogacies were approved in Ireland each year and that almost all these were to opposite-sex couples with fertility difficulties, for whom it represented the last or only available option in assisted human reproduction; that surrogacy should and would be regulated; and that this regulation and the availability of surrogacy would not be influenced one way or the other by the passage of the constitutional amendment.

The third No poster had no photography but simply the words 'We Already Have Civil Partnership; Don't Redefine Marriage. Vote No'. It touched on one of the sensitive vulnerabilities for the Yes campaign. Could the availability of civil partnership now get in the way of securing marriage equality? Some of the early polling suggested that it might.

Yes Equality could not afford its own ongoing market research so, when the *Sunday Business Post* published its first Red C poll during the actual campaign on Sunday 1st May, Yes campaigners devoured the detail. The headline figures were still good at 72 per cent Yes among likely voters. They knew it overstated the probable Yes vote somewhat, but the key point was that there had been no significant shift. However, the *Sunday Business Post*, working with political scientists David Farrell, Theresa Reidy and Jane Suiter, who were all conducting a referendum study, also asked some more detailed questions about issues that were likely to arise in the campaign. One of those questions was whether the respondent agreed or disagreed with the statement, 'Children have always been central to marriage. It is inappropriate for children to be raised by gay couples'. Interestingly, 67 per cent of respondents disagreed. However, they also asked respondents whether they agreed or disagreed with the following suggestion: 'Same-sex couples have full legal protection and can enter State-recognised civil partnerships. There is no need to go further and completely change the definition of marriage'. Forty-six per cent of poll respondents agreed with the statement. For Yes Equality, that was very worrying.

Again the lines to take in response to the notion that Civil Partnership was enough had been developed well in advance of the campaign. This poll information spurred Yes Equality to fine-tune its argument. The best approach was to emphasise again and again the distinct societal, legal and constitutional status and protection which attaches to marriage, and the sense of exclusion which civil partnership communicates to same-sex couples and to the gay and lesbian community generally.

The campaign had been warned, however, by Thalia Zepatos from Freedom to Marry and others, not to get bogged down in the statutory differences. In other countries marriage equality opponents had successfully countered this by promising to redress these differences by legislation. Yes Equality knew that in Ireland such a suggestion could be fatal to a proposal for constitutional change.

The argument that Yes Equality began to use more and more was to emphasise the societal difference between civil partnership and marriage and the discrimination felt by lesbian and gay couples locked out by the Constitution from the option of getting married. Voters, and not just married voters, knew that marriage was different from partnership. They knew that getting married was a different step and statement. Both these aspects of the messages were emphasised and honed in a series of statements and speeches made by the campaign. An *Irish Times* column by Noel, under the headline 'What's the difference between Marriage and Civil Partnership' got very wide attention online and became a hymn sheet for politicians and others looking for the language and concepts that best illustrated the real and symbolic differences.

Overall, the No posters had a galvanising effect on the Yes campaign at just the right moment. They provoked many Yes supporters out of their complacency. Yes Equality headquarters decided to take advantage of this response, with messages such as 'Don't get angry – Donate', or 'Don't get angry – Canvass'. Online donations to fund Yes posters and enquiries to the Yes campaign from those volunteering to canvass soared in the days after the No posters were first published. Some €24,000 was raised online in the first twenty-four hours. The No posters were also mercilessly parodied online, which became a helpful antidote to the distress many felt on seeing them.

After the posters went up, the bishops' letters were sent out and the arguments, although made less crudely, were essentially the same. One early strategic error on the part of the Yes Equality campaign was that it underestimated the extent and intensity with which the Catholic Church leadership would get involved on the No side. The bishops came in earlier and more stridently than had originally been anticipated. On Saturday 2nd May Yes Equality were taken by surprise when RTÉ TV news carried a story about a message to the faithful from the Archbishop of Armagh, Eamon Martin, which was to be read at churches that weekend. The RTÉ news bulletin had no response from the Yes side.

A quick exchange of texts meant that Brian, Gráinne, Noel and Cathy had what was to be their only unscheduled conference call of the campaign as soon as that news bulletin ended. Cathy and Noel both came on the line furious. Their language was colourful. They were angry not just at the fact that the timing of the bishops' intervention meant they would have three full Sundays to hammer home their opposition, but they were also furious at the tone of the archbishop's statement. The insinuations in the statement were deeply offensive to gay and lesbian people and their families, and not less so because the wording used was very subtle. Brian and Gráinne were calmer; if anything they were entertained by Noel and Cathy's reaction. For decades they had had to listen to the same insulting argument from the Catholic Church. Lesbian and gay people were almost immune to it. The Catholic Church had vigorously opposed all major progress for lesbian and gay people. They had campaigned against decriminalisation of homosexuality and against civil partnership. Indeed, the then Cardinal and Primate of All Ireland, Seán Brady, threatened in 2008 to go all the way to the Supreme Court to challenge civil partnership if the Oireachtas passed the legislation.

Noel suggested the idea of a head-on confrontation with the hierarchy for its failure to distinguish between civil and religious marriage. It would certainly have mobilised the grassroots and given a more identifiable enemy with which to engage. Cathy initially warmed to the idea, but Gráinne and Brian talked them down. Marriage Equality and GLEN had always rejected suggestions that the Catholic Church was not entitled to comment on civil law issues relating to gay and lesbian rights. Their approach had been to respect the Church's right to speak while strongly disagreeing with its argument.

Ultimately, their collective assessment was that the bishops would have little impact on middle-ground support. The four of them decided to issue a statement in time for the *Nine O'Clock News* bulletin that would express disappointment at the tone of the Archbishop's intervention and invite him and other bishops into a dialogue with Yes Equality about the referendum. Gráinne went into RTÉ studios that Monday morning and invited the Archbishop, now that he had entered the public debate, to publicly discuss with Yes Equality the matters he had raised on air. They knew of course that the bishops would never take up the offer to debate, but challenging them highlighted the hierarchy's unwillingness to engage on the issue.

The bishops again took to the pulpits and airwaves in opposition to the referendum on the following two Sundays. Their campaign was professionally run by communications advisers and by the hierarchy's press office, which each Saturday evening or Sunday morning issued staggered press releases drawing attention to the key lines in each letter from the different bishops. In reality the Catholic Church was the largest campaigning organisation in the referendum, at least on the No side, with its opportunity to deliver unchallenged messages to tens of thousands of mass-goers each weekend.

If the Catholic bishops' position couldn't be challenged within the churches, then Yes Equality was determined that it would not again go unchallenged in the media. The approach of a respectful response to the bishops' pronouncements and calls for real dialogue was maintained throughout the campaign. This was supplemented by spotlighting the many statements from individual priests and religious who announced that they were voting Yes. Among those who made thoughtful contributions to the referendum in that regard were the social justice campaigner Father Peter McVerry in Dublin, the Augustian Priest, Father Iggy O'Donovan, now in Limerick, the theologian, Father Tony Flannery and Father Pádraig Standún, a columnist with the *Connacht Tribune*. Sister Stanislaus Kennedy put her position as follows: 'I have thought a lot about this. I am going to vote Yes in recognition of the gay community as full members of society. They should have an entitlement to marry. It is a civil right and a human right.' In Cork Father Tim

Hazelwood spoke of how 'gay people deserve the same rights as everyone else' while Father Brian Ó Fearraigh in Donegal, expressed similar sentiments. The words of these compassionate clergy and others who spoke of their faith, such as Ursula Halligan and Tom Curran, had successfully undermined any influence the bishops might have had beyond their core flock. The eloquence and bravery with which so many of them spoke was impressive. It also had real influence.

Yes Equality also took heart from many individual stories that reached them about disquiet among Catholic Church congregations at the manner in which the hierarchy and some priests were approaching the referendum. Earlier in the year Father Martin Dolan of St Nicholas of Myra parish on Frances Street in Dublin, instead of giving a sermon seeking a No vote, talked to the congregation about why they should vote Yes. He finished by saying that he himself was a gay man. The congregation gave him a spontaneous standing ovation. There were also many reports in the regional media, including Enniscorthy and Donegal, of people walking out of the church when the sermons by the priests were particularly trenchant in seeking a No vote.

The issues raised in the No posters, and to a lesser extent those in the bishops' letters, framed and in some instances even determined the nature and content of the various media contests over the following four weeks.

The first big media debate was that held on *The Late Late Show* on Friday 1st May. The show's producers themselves selected the Yes contributors. They were looking for campaigners with interesting personal stories. For the Yes side they settled ultimately on Colm O'Gorman and Una Mullally. The No speakers were to be Keith Mills and Petra Conroy, a spokesperson from Catholic Comment.

Contrary to some perceptions, Yes Equality did not have control over who the panellists on the Yes side were for most of the media debates, but when they knew who the programmes had selected, they invited them in to discuss what messages should be emphasised. Noel led these gatherings, with input from Cathy,

Brian and Gráinne, and on occasion there was outside help from the communication consultant Donal Cronin, who, on a pro bono basis, acted as another sounding board for the campaign. They knew they couldn't tell other speakers what they should say or how they should say it. Many of the leading proponents of marriage equality were strong independent personalities. Noel, Brian, Gráinne and Cathy knew that these advocates would take on board the messages suggested by the campaign only if they were intellectually persuaded of the merits of the arguments and the good campaign reasons for adopting a calm and moderate tone.

Colm and Una came by for a briefing a few hours before *The Late Late Show*. The group found them very well prepared. They were both passionate and competent on the issue. They had met up a couple of days previously themselves to co-ordinate their approach. They were both very conscious of the need to assuage the apprehensions of mainstream voters. *The Late Late Show* always had a very large audience, most of whom would be hearing the referendum arguments for the first time. Colm was a seasoned media performer and recognised that, as well as making the human rights case for marriage equality as Director of Amnesty International Ireland, he would be expected, since this was also a light entertainment programme, to talk about his own family situation. At the briefing, Una spoke of how she had been disappointed in her own performance on a *Claire Byrne Live* debate about marriage equality the previous January. This time, however, she was not going to be provoked by the other side; she was clearly, and for obvious reasons after her cancer diagnosis, in a more reflective place, but her passion about her and her partner Sarah's right to equality was all the more determined.

The format for the segment on *The Late Late Show* that night involved the host Ryan Tubridy doing a short one-on-one interview with each of the speakers. Each then made an opening statement from a podium and that was followed by a debate. Colm and Una did extraordinarily well in all aspects of the encounter. The last part of the segment involved questions and answers with people on both sides of the issue in the audience. This proved scrappy and at times tetchy, although for the Yes side there were key audience contributions, including one from Grania Long from the ISPCC.

Colm's and Una's performances on *The Late Late Show* drew uniformly positive comments in the media, online and on the doorsteps.

The next outing was less clear-cut. RTÉ's main current affairs programme, *Prime Time,* had scheduled the first of their two televised debates for Tuesday 5th May. The format and line-up for this event changed several times in the days before. The producers had agreed that they would include one minister, who the government had decided would be Justice Minister Frances Fitzgerald, and one Yes Equality speaker. The third speaker for the Yes side, *Prime Time* told Cathy, had still to be decided.

This brought to a head an ongoing discussion within Yes Equality about who should be the designated spokesperson for the campaign. The communications team had already identified a series of mainstream voices with established profiles who had written endorsements or opinion pieces. There was a concern, however, that, although supportive and articulate, these personalities would not be comfortable or competent enough on the referendum issues in the volatile environment of intense broadcast debate. It was an ongoing frustration for the Yes Equality communications team that sometimes even those politicians who were committed on the issue came across as ill-informed, intemperate or both.

A decision was also made that the campaign needed its own identifiable voice and, while there were several options among those who had previously been spokespersons for either GLEN or Marriage Equality or ICCL, it was felt that Gráinne was the best person to become that lead public face. The campaign needed an authoritative female voice. Gráinne was deeply absorbed in the detail of the issues, was strongly committed to the more moderate messaging, and, as a lesbian woman who had recently become a grandmother, she could speak to her personal experience. It was also decided that Gráinne should take the Yes Equality spot in the *Prime Time* and other debates and that Brian would speak publicly on campaign matters, including the Get Out the Vote campaign.

Yes Equality also needed to identify straight spokespersons, especially straight male voices. Fergus Finlay was an obvious choice and he had the added advantage of being a leading advocate for children's rights as Chief Executive of Barnardos. Peter Ward was also pencilled in for future media appearances; he had performed a similar role during the second divorce referendum and was comfortable with the legal and political issues around marriage equality. In these discussions about the need for straight males who could best articulate the case for marriage equality to middle-aged men in particular, Cathy kept pointing out that another obvious answer was sitting in front of them in the form of Noel Whelan himself. Noel had, the previous week, done an hour-long debate with fellow columnist Breda O'Brien on an *Irish Times* podcast which had gone well for the Yes side.

He was reluctant, however, to become a front of house face for the campaign. He had got involved on the basis that not seeking a spokesperson role for himself would give him a greater impact in shaping who would be put out and seek to persuade them in what they might say. Cathy persisted and Brian, agreeing that he himself would stay in the background, was given the task of persuading Noel to be an advocate on broadcast media.

The question of Noel's going out front was finally resolved the Friday before the debate when the *Prime Time* editor rang to say that on the Yes side, in addition to Minister Fitzgerald and Gráinne, they were going to ask Noel to come on the panel. It seems the decision was shaped by the reaction to his column about the difference between civil partnership and marriage, which had appeared in the *Irish Times* that morning.

Right up until the day, it was not clear who the No speakers would be. In a tactic that was repeated for each debate, the No side left it until late to tell producers whom they would field. It seemed to depend on who their opponents were or what issue they wanted to focus on. In the end the line-up on the No side was David Quinn, Eileen King and the columnist and commentator John Waters.

On the Tuesday afternoon the Iona Institute published a 140-page legal opinion which they claimed confirmed that if the referendum was passed, it would not be possible for a future government to distinguish between opposite-sex couples and same-sex couples in adoption or surrogacy. Mark Kelly led the effort on developing a rapid point by point response to the Iona claims. Early on Tuesday evening Noel, Gráinne, Brian and Cathy met with Frances Fitzgerald to go through what might come up. The Minister was comfortable with the issues after recently shepherding the Child and Family Relationships Bill through the Houses of the Oireachtas. They agreed that they should all stay calm, remain unprovoked and keep the focus on the equality aspect of the argument and on the real lives that would be affected.

After this briefing, Cathy and Brian travelled to the RTÉ studios with Gráinne and Noel. The mood in the Green Room before the debate was polite but tense. Both sides exchanged the usual pleasantries but then kept to their own side of the room. The atmosphere reflected the intensity of the issues at stake.

The debate itself was knockabout stuff. The two sides were seated without desks facing each other, with *Prime Time* presenter David McCullagh in the middle. The format, the number of speakers, and indeed some of the personalities involved did not lend itself to a calm exposition of the issues. The No speakers went almost immediately into adoption and surrogacy and at times it was difficult for McCullagh to keep order. Frances Fitzgerald opened for the Yes side by pointing out that marriage had evolved over time, that it was a complement to marriage that same-sex couples wished to avail of it and that the referendum was asking the people to give access to marriage and the constitutional protections which it provides to all equally. Gráinne's strongest input was to remind viewers of the reality that children were already being reared, and reared well in lesbian- or gay-headed households. As she put it in her most memorable question: 'These children already exist. What are we to do with them? Send them to Mars?' Noel surprised many with his passion on the issue. He pointed out that if his young son turned out to be gay, then he would 'kick in every door in the land' to ensure he got full equality, in all aspects of his life, including his marriage. Noel also repeated the point he had made in his column on the distinction between marriage and civil partnership and again used the analogy that if he introduces his wife, everyone knows where she stands in relation to him in society and there is no uncertainty at hospital A&E or in other scenarios where next of kin issues arise. Rather than get bogged down in the legal argument about the Iona opinion, he emphasised that passing the referendum would ensure an end to discrimination and that the future which Quinn and others were arguing for, was a future of inequality.

Coming out of the studio, Gráinne and Noel thought the debate had gone well but when they met up in the foyer of the RTÉ television building they found Brian and Cathy less enthused. The other two felt the No side had successfully managed to stoke fear about surrogacy and adoption and that Quinn's and Waters's constant interruptions had minimised the opportunity to get the key Yes messages across.

As well as being focused on getting the best out of the debate behind the scenes, the Yes Equality team was also trying to stop one debate, the very idea of which was not in the interest of the Yes campaign. Breda O'Brien, in an interview with the *Sunday Independent* on the 20th April, had challenged Panti Bliss to a head-to-head debate on the referendum. Her challenge led to a colourful *Independent.ie* front page featuring the two of them dressed in striking red. The idea worried the Yes Equality communications team. Rory O'Neill, as his Panti alter ego and otherwise, had made a significant contribution to the marriage equality struggle over the years, not least in her Noble Call address from the stage of the Abbey Theatre a year earlier. He was also an incredibly astute and intelligent communicator and likely to come out best in any encounter with Breda O'Brien. However, the notion of Breda baiting Panti into a debate risked exactly the kind of caricature that everyone on the Yes side was anxious to avoid during the campaign. Apart from anything else, such a debate would become the title fight of the campaign, and would suck up media coverage and attention for days before and afterwards. If for any reason it went wrong, it would be a game changer for the No side, and sitting on a comfortable lead in the polls, Yes Equality knew they didn't need that.

Rory O'Neill himself appreciated this. He was abroad on tour for some of the campaign but even when in Ireland he had decided to maintain a low media profile. Panti focused instead on communicating key messages to the core community audience and with 52,000 Facebook followers and almost as many Twitter followers, she was well placed to do so. Rory put in much effort in these weeks monitoring the comment feed on Panti's accounts in both social media outlets, anxious to play his part in ensuring that a moderate tone was maintained. He also spent a lot of time canvassing, which gave him a real sense of the mood on the ground, and acted as a great morale boost to those Yes Equality groups he visited. In addition he kept in close contact with Brian to discuss how he could best contribute to the campaign effort. They both agreed that in the crucial last weeks, less was best when it came to media opportunities.

Rory was very shrewd in his reply to Breda's challenge. He couldn't be seen to duck it but was live to the risk that speculation about such a bout might trivialise the referendum. He tweeted an acceptance of her offer but told the various programme producers who were tripping over themselves to host such a debate that he would do it only as Rory O'Neill and not as Panti. When the broadcasters relayed Rory's offer back to Breda, there was a delay before she replied telling them she was unwell. She ultimately declined to participate. The producers for Brendan O'Connor's *Saturday Night Show* were so anxious to host the showdown that they encouraged Rory to send her a tweet accusing her of being chicken so as to provoke her to participate. Rory politely declined.

The next actual media debate was on the Monday night's *Claire Byrne Live* show. The format here was a head-to-head debate between Minister Simon Coveney and the Independent Senator Ronan Mullen. After about twenty minutes of just the two of them, the debate was to be broadened to involve an invited audience, again made up of representatives of various groups involved on both sides of the campaign.

Since they did not have a speaker on the panel, the focus for Yes Equality HQ was to identify good contributors of their own for the audience, reach out to other groups who had been invited to provide audience participants and offer any assistance that might be of use to Simon Coveney.

The Minister spent most of that Monday afternoon preparing for the debate. Mary O'Toole SC and Peter Ward SC, who were to be in the audience from Lawyers for Yes, met with him early Monday evening and Noel tagged along. They found the Minister focused. They discussed topics likely to come up, in particular on the legal issues. At the end of their chat, the Minister said that in the previous weeks, as Director of the Fine Gael campaign, he had come to truly appreciate how much the referendum mattered to gay and lesbian people and their families. 'I have never felt so nervous before a television programme in my life,' he said. 'This issue really matters to so many.'

The Minister held his own in the debate. His message was clearly targeted at middle-ground voters. Mullen was the best debater the No campaign put out; an accomplished rhetorician and a barrister, he had a better feel for the electorate than many others in the No campaign. Again, when it went to the audience, the debate got scrappy but it included another strong contribution from Grainia Long of ISPCC.

On that night, however, the most important contribution did not come from any of the speakers for either side but from an interview in a film report in the middle of the programme with Geoffrey Shannon, the child law expert and chairman of the Adoption Authority of Ireland. He explained that there had been 112 adoptions in Ireland the previous year and pointed out that irrespective of whether the applicant was a sole applicant, a married couple, a cohabiting couple, or a same-sex couple, 'the assessment looks at your capacity to parent a child into adulthood. It is not concerned with gender or sexual orientation'. He also emphasised that birth mothers are centrally involved in the decision about the placement of a child and actually determine who the child is placed with. Above all else, he emphasised, 'Whether you vote Yes or No on the 22nd May, the adoption process is not going to change.' It was an important contribution, giving the lie to many of the inaccuracies that the No side were promulgating about adoption and marriage equality.

Another key moment came at the end of the programme when RTÉ put up a graphic with the details of an Amárach Poll commissioned by the programme. It showed 76 per cent for the Yes side. Although the debate itself had at times been very confusing, this seemed to tell viewers that, despite all the concerns raised by Mullen and others, most of their fellow voters were inclined to vote Yes.

In the following days there were a series of significant interventions from the chairman of the Referendum Commission, Judge Kevin Cross, who, when again pressed on the issue of surrogacy, made it clear that the issue had nothing to do with the referendum.

What Geoffrey Shannon and Justice Cross were saying about adoption and surrogacy was what the Yes campaign had been saying for months, but it was crucially now being said in the heat of the referendum debate by authoritative independent voices.

At this stage in the campaign, Yes Equality's relationship with RTÉ was becoming strained. Cathy, Brian, Gráinne and Noel had met with RTÉ in mid-April as part of a round of meetings with newspaper and broadcast editors before the campaign properly started. The purpose was to introduce Yes Equality and identify Cathy as the key contact for the main political coverage and debates. In these discussions with broadcasters, Yes Equality sought to encourage them away from the Punch and Judy formats towards more interview or exposition pieces with each side and independent reportage on the issues. They found the broadcasters resistant to altering the traditional approach. In fact, RTÉ's approach in their coverage of the marriage referendum involved less independent assessment of the issues as the public service broadcaster than had been the case in previous referendums. During various European referendums, for example, RTÉ political staff covered the campaign, while their European Correspondent performed the function of explaining to voters the various treaty provisions or other issues. Seán Whelan, when in that role, had operated as an independent in-studio expert on some of the claims and counter-claims.

In the marriage equality referendum, however, there was little effort by RTÉ to perform this function. Even though the controversies about surrogacy and adoption, for example, raged for weeks, there was no use of the health correspondent or the social affairs correspondent to explain the factual situation. Coverage mainly took the form of 'one side says this, the other side says that' reports. The Yes Equality communications team, like their counterparts on the other side, were of course closely monitoring the amount of time allocated to each side in coverage, but their main concern was with the tendency of some presenters to repeat the No side proposition as questions and to give much time to asking Yes speakers to respond to issues which, it was now clear, were unaffected by the referendum.

There was a real sense among the Yes Equality communication team that RTÉ had been spooked by the Pantigate controversy a year earlier and was now overcompensating. Even if the Yes campaign was not objective enough to assess whether or not this led to unfair coverage, it was clear to all that the RTÉ coverage was conservative and unimaginative.

One particularly galling indication of this tendency was the realisation that even though the *Claire Byrne Show*, to its credit, had gone to Geoffrey Shannon for an independent opinion as Chairman of the Adoption Authority of Ireland, RTÉ appeared to have counted the whole of his time on screen in the programme as time given to the Yes argument.

These tensions between Yes Equality and RTÉ played out in correspondence between the campaign and RTÉ's in-house steering committee for referendum coverage, but to little avail. Similar correspondence flew, it seems, between RTÉ and the No campaign, which the latter took to copying to the Broadcasting Authority of Ireland. Yes Equality could, of course, have complained publicly, but that would have proved counterproductive in the short term, and been inconsistent with the overall positive positioning of the campaign. So they decided to just absorb it.

What was reassuring for the campaign was the feedback the Yes side was getting from canvass returns around the country. The support for marriage equality was holding and it had not been shifted by the TV and radio debates. At this stage, with thousands of canvassers out nightly and at weekends, it was clear to all in Clarendon Street that Yes Equality was winning the 'ground war'. On social media the Yes campaign was not just winning but buzzing with activity and excitement. The Yes side might only be holding its own in the 'air war' on the broadcast media, but that was enough. The sense from the feedback to campaign headquarters was that, although people were watching and listening to the broadcast encounters in large numbers, they were not swayed much by them.

What Yes Equality was hearing from their canvassers was consistent with the details of an earlier Amárach poll for the *Claire Byrne Show*, which the presenter had blogged about a week earlier. That poll asked people not only how they would vote in the referendum but also whether they had changed their minds in the previous seven days. The question was asked after the first week of debates on *The Late Late Show* and *Prime Time* and on various radio programmes. Only 9 per cent said they had changed and, of those, half had switched from Yes to No and half had shifted from No to Yes. The intensive phase of at times noisy media debates had little impact on most voters.

If this was the sense among the Yes Equality communications and mobilisation teams, it was not shared by others involved in the campaign. The barrage of argument about adoption, surrogacy and civil partnership led many to fear that the campaign was not being robust enough in countering the No side assertions, that all the momentum appeared to be with the No campaign, and even that the referendum could slip away. Lawyers for Yes and others involved in the campaign wanted to counter these No arguments more robustly.

The campaign was also coming under mounting pressure from some of its LGBT supporters to go out fighting to defend LGBT people against the No side's attacks.

These concerns were fuelled by almost incessant media speculation about a so-called 'silent' No vote. Indeed, throughout the campaign it was noticeable that most of the political correspondents and political commentators were ill-informed about what was happening on the ground. They seemed to be relying entirely on chitchat from backbench politicians from the main parties in Leinster House, many of whom were opposed to or had lukewarm feelings towards the proposal, and most of whom were not canvassing at all. On this slim basis, several political correspondents and other commentators in print, on radio and on podcast, talked up the supposed existence of this silent No vote. The reality, as Yes Equality knew from its groups around the country, was very different. One of the few political correspondents to see this was Harry McGee of the *Irish Times,* who had not only visited Yes Equality headquarters but had also gone out canvassing with both Yes and No canvassers in Mullingar for a video blog and an online piece he did on the campaign. The twenty Yes Equality volunteers he went out with included Sandra's sister and her husband. McGee spotted early on the effect which canvassers telling personal stories, or setting out their reasons for voting Yes, was having on the doorsteps and on the overall campaign. Even before going to Mullingar, he told Gráinne how he had realised something different was going on the previous weekend when getting a train at Heuston Station. There was a Yes Equality crew handing out leaflets to people rushing for trains saying 'I'm voting yes, can I tell you why?' and people stopped to listen to the story of why the canvasser was voting yes and take the leaflet. He had never seen anything like it in his many years of reporting on campaigns. Gráinne later discovered that the canvassers in Heuston on the evening in question had been from Yes Equality Dublin South Central and had included Noel Sutton, director of the Gaze Film Festival. She passed this on to Noel and his team.

Those within the campaign who expressed concern about the impact of the media debates were not basing this on the views of political reporters but rather on anecdotal feedback, in some instances from their own canvassing and their own overall sense of how the campaign was going. People like Peter Ward, who had previously seen the lead in the second divorce referendum almost slip away, warned of the dangers of leaving No arguments unanswered.

The matter came to a head at an untypically tense meeting of the Advisory Group on Tuesday 12th May. At this early-morning gathering, Peter and Mark Kelly were strongest on the need for a more active rebuttal while Fergus Finlay and Martin Mackin were most vocal among those arguing for the campaign to hold its course.

In reply, Noel explained that he was open to advising a more robust strategy if it emerged in polling the following weekend that the current approach of calm positivity and personal stories was not working. He warned of falling into the trap of reverting to a tone that would enable the No side, and lazy media, to characterise the Yes campaign as nasty. If there was to be a shift in strategy, he argued, it had to be evidence-based and all the evidence they had, incomplete though it was because of the absence of polls, suggested that the current strategy was working. The canvass reports were strong, even when discounting for the political inexperience of some canvassers and putting all 'Don't Knows' down as No voters. The fundraising was really taking off. The party general secretaries had told them that they believed that the Yes vote was holding up, as had those government politicians who might have had access to their own polling. Noel joked about how the previous day Brian had a call from Government Buildings saying that the Taoiseach wanted to get involved in more Yes Equality events, which was a real sign of growing government confidence about the outcome.

However, Mark and Peter expressed concern that waiting for a shift in polls might be too late to change tack, and indeed that the polls might be missing the shift. Noel feared, unfairly perhaps, that they might just be exhibiting a lawyer's instinct to want to win an argument rather than shore up support.

The Yes Equality HQ Crew: Staff and volunteers from the Yes Equality headquarters, bus, shop and distribution teams. (Photo: Paul McCarthy/*Gay Community News*). See appendix for full index to those photographed.

You Can Let Me Marry Too: (L:R) David Caron, Sandra Irwin-Gowran, Celeste Roche, John Curran, Sarah Gilligan pose with Yes Equality's final poster featuring each of them on Grafton Street, 15th May 2015. (Photo: Sharpix)

Fathers For Yes: Martin McAleese, Tom Curran and Ashok Varadkar pictured with Yes Equality canvassers outside the GPO on O'Connell Street, Dublin to mark the launch of National Canvass Day, 16th May 2015. (Photo: Sharpix)

Closing Argument: Mary McAleese addresses BeLong To Yes event at the Wood Quay Venue, Dublin, 19th May 2015. (Photo: Marc O'Sullivan/BeLonG To Youth Services)

'I'd Be Delighted': 85 year-old Vivian Sheehan agrees to accept the 500,000th Yes Equality badge from Brian and Gráinne on Grafton Street, Dublin, 20th May 2015. (Photo: Sharpix)

Yes Equality's Final Photo Call: Craig Dwyer (on top) and other staff and campaigners pose for the final Yes Equality photocall, 21st May 2015. (Photo: Peter Morrison/AP/PA Images)

Annie West @anniewestdotcom · May 22
#marref #hometovote
1.3K   1.1K

#hometovote: Illustrator Annie West tweets her sketch depicting crowds coming into Dublin airport on the evening before the referendum. It was retweeted 2,700 times in six hours, 22nd May 2015.

It's A Yes Landslide!: Senator David Norris is welcomed by Andrew Hyland as he arrives at the Dublin count centre at the RDS Dublin, 23rd May 2015. (Photo: Brian Lawless/AP/PA Images)

 Sebastian Enke @S_Enke · May 23
.@goggshealy @brianatglen and @noelwhelan arriving at Count Centre @TheRDS ! #MarRef

↩   ⇄ 2   ★ 4   •••

A Very Sunny Saturday: (L:R) Noel, Gráinne, Brian and Cathy Madden are captured by tweeter Sebastian Enke just before they enter the RDS count centre, 23rd May 2015.

Joy At The Castle: Panti Bliss pictured among the carnival Yes atmosphere at Dublin Castle, 23rd May 2013. (Photo: Paul Faith/Getty Images)

Marriage Equality At Last: Katherine Zappone and Ann Louise Gilligan at Dublin Castle for the referendum result, 23rd May 2015. (Photo: Clodagh Kilcoyne/Getty Images)

 Dearbhail McDonald @DearbhailDibs · May 23
A teary @noelwhelan mobbed outside #DublinCastle #MarRef

↩   ⟳ 41   ★ 93   •••

Thanks For Advocating For Us: Dearbhail McDonald captures Noel's teary moment on Dame Street, 23rd May 2015.

Christov @redmondch1 · May 26
#WeMadeHistory #MarRef - yes equality cork hq 23.05.2015

↩   ⟳ 1   ★ 3   •••

It's Done!: Cork Yes Equality headquarters team celebrate the result in Cork, where all but 10 boxes across the county voted Yes, 23rd May 2015.

Westmeath Says Yes: The referendum result was big news internationally, nationally and locally, including on the front page of the *Westmeath Examiner*, 30th May 2015 (courtesy *Westmeath Examiner*)

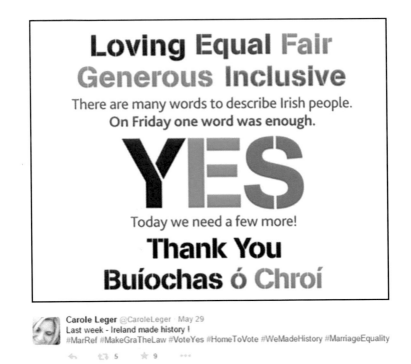

Thank You: A prolific tweeter Carole Leger retweets Yes Equality's final message to voters, 29th May 2015.

Mark Garrett, who chaired this meeting, agreed with Noel and Fergus, but he persuaded the group to compromise, shaped in part by a view from Cathy, Brian and Gráinne that there was a need to rebut some of the issues raised by the No campaign which still lingered in the debate. If this needed to be done, however, it was agreed that it must be without compromising the positive approach. This they felt could best be achieved by a panel of authoritative voices who, in addition to giving their own view as experts for the Yes campaign, could reiterate what independent people like Geoffrey Shannon and Judge Kevin Cross had said.

It was agreed that a 'panel of experts' event would be put together, as well as specific rebuttal initiatives co-ordinated by the ICCL and Lawyers for Yes. This press conference, which was entitled 'Nothing but the Truth' was held on Thursday 15th May. It was held in the larger room in Clarendon Street, which had now been fitted out as a press conference centre, and a reworked rebuttal document prepared by Mark Kelly was launched to coincide with it.

The event proved crucial in shifting the campaign mood. The speakers were Fergus Finlay as a children's rights advocate, Peter Ward as a Senior Counsel and Maureen Gaffney. Maureen, as a psychologist, author and social commentator, had solid appeal to the mainstream as well as an established capacity to persuasively address popular concerns about social change.

Together, these speakers robustly tackled the No campaign for its scaremongering and encouraged voters to consider the real issue. Fergus accused the No side of 'peddling the politics of fear' by what he called 'cynical and dishonest tactics' to scare the electorate. Fergus had arrived at the event with a large blue IKEA bag full of books on parenting, and at this point he plonked them up in front of journalists, saying that in none of the studies in the books, which represented the best literature on parenting over the last ten or fifteen years, 'in not one', had any research said that lesbian or gay parents were any worse than straight parents, and that the indications were that the opposite was true.

Maureen reframed the question of family, parenting and children by asking what it was that those opposed to marriage equality were actually afraid of. She asked them to name their fears. No piece of peer-reviewed research on this issue since the 1970s had ever said there was anything damaging to children in lesbian- and gay-headed families. She went on later that day to make the same points very effectively on a special *Drivetime* radio debate.

At the press conference Peter emphasised that not only Lawyers for Yes and the ICCL, but also the Chairman of the Referendum Commission and the Adoption Authority had shown why issues like adoption and surrogacy were not relevant to the referendum. 'A legal pathway has now been cleared,' he said, 'to focus on the central issue, the equality-issue whether gay and lesbian people should be constitutionally entitled to marry.' He captured the sense that questions had been asked and answered, that reasonable concerns had been listened to and addressed, that those with apprehensions had been given the space to voice them and had been reassured and that voters could now focus on whether to share the freedom to marry with gay and lesbian couples in the interest of equality.

While all these issues and arguments were consuming mainstream media, Yes Equality, as well as implementing a more extensive canvassing strategy, was driving intense and highly visual coverage on social media.

Yes Equality was unapologetic about its cultivation of celebrity support for the campaign because it enabled them to access audiences not usually interested in politics. Some of the celebrity endorsements were initiated by contacts made by members of the Clarendon Street team. Others happened spontaneously. The communications team liaised with the *Daily Mail* about a magazine story in which Majella O'Donnell would call for a Yes Vote. A few days before the edition appeared, however, Daniel O'Donnell was asked during a general interview on radio with Ray D'Arcy what he made of the referendum. The Donegal man replied that 'those who know what they're talking about are saying that families won't change'. 'I think everyone should be equal.' It was a terrific boost to the Yes campaign.

Many of the endorsements from celebrities were in the form of specially made videos. There were literally hundreds of them. By far the most impactful of these was *Mrs Brown's Address to the Nation*, made by famous director Lenny Abrahamson and promoter Buzz O'Neill with the comedian Brendan O'Carroll. They shot specially scripted footage for the video, on set in Scotland. As well as being highly entertaining, the script cleverly reinforced the key message about how every mother wanted equality for each of her children.

The video was launched in early May by the actor Rory Cowan at a special event to mark the opening of a Yes Equality Pop-Up Shop in St Stephen's Green. The opening of the shop was just the latest development in the phenomenal success of the Yes Equality merchandising operation. Patrick Sweeney and his team just about managed to keep the distribution centre stocked to meet the incredible demand for Yes Equality wearables. The St Stephen's Green shop was staffed entirely by volunteers and became a mecca for those looking for badges, posters and t-shirts. It also became a magnet for well-wishers and for those just wanting to be close to the activity or merely to chat about the campaign. In addition, it was a significant fundraiser and flagship. Every evening there were new stories from the shop. Tourists and natives alike loved the TÁ badges and t-shirts. A Mayo woman living in Australia dropped in to buy t-shirts and other merchandise on her way home in order to canvass her village. Among the foreign visitors looking for the high-visibility vest was a man from the American space agency NASA. At the same time, another team led by Gabbi Mastromatteo were dealing with a surge in demand in the online store, much of it from abroad. In all, the Yes Equality merchandising department sold 6,500 t-Shirts, 2,300 tote bags and 800 high-visibility jackets. By mid-May 2015 Yes Equality had also shifted about 450,000 TÁ or Yes badges.

The variety of recognisable images that emerged was illustrative of how this campaign was like no previous campaign, particularly with regard to its visual impact. A gigantic mural by the artist Joe Caslin of two men embracing, applied to the side of a four-storey building at the corner of South George's Street in Dublin, became the most posted and retweeted image of the campaign, reaching an online audience hundreds of times the size of that which saw it when passing on the street. A second mural by Caslin, depicting two women in a tender pose installed in Caher Castle in Craughwell, County Galway, also went viral.

The creative talent available to the campaign was also illustrated by a special event entitled *A Noble Call For Marriage Equality*, hosted by Senator Fiach MacConghail and Councillor Mannix Flynn at the Abbey Theatre on the 13th May. During the seventy-minute show some of the country's leading actors, writers and performers read poems, sang songs or gave short orations in support of the Yes Campaign. Among those who took to the stage were satirist Oliver Callan, actor Gabriel Byrne, writer Roddy Doyle and playwrights Marina Carr and Frank McGuinness.

The viral and visual impact of the Yes Equality's campaign was greatly assisted by the efforts of Karl Hayden, a long-time human rights campaigner and gay activist who volunteered as a full-time video producer for the last three weeks of the campaign. Karl and his camera recorded all the events and happenings of the campaign. He also developed a makeshift studio and editing suite at Clarendon Street, from which, as well as making the daily Yes Equality vlog, Karl and a team of volunteer editors working full-time produced numerous other high-quality campaign videos. Karl was also responsible for setting up the professional conference facility at Clarendon Street, which was favourably commented upon by media practitioners, especially videographers and photographers used to grappling with the problems of poor acoustics and bad lighting. Karl's efforts were supplemented by a steady stream of spontaneously generated videos from partner organisations and individual activists. One day Brian opened his inbox to find an email from Andy Bradford of Sweet Media and the Irish International Advertising Agency with a link to a terrific video targeted at a younger male audience which they had made for the campaign, featuring the actor Laurence Kinlan, best known for the role of Elmo in the crime drama *Love Hate*.

After reviewing several of the campaign videos at one advisory meeting, Fergus Finlay was driven to comment, 'Whatever about anything else, I am certain about one think after this campaign. The gays and their friends make the best videos.'

If the Yes Equality campaign had a strong showreel, it also had a lively soundtrack. Several artists and musicians supported the campaign and many offered specially recorded or previously released songs. Yvonne Judge used her contacts to secure permission for the use of Snow Patrol's 'Just Say Yes'. The band's international management had refused permission for use of the song in the Scottish Independence referendum and the song was taken off playlists in Scotland for the duration of the campaign. Gary Lightbody of Snow Patrol was an enthusiastic supporter of the Yes Equality campaign. The band published a special video wishing the campaign well and, as an anthem, 'Just Say Yes' proved a big hit.

Musical performers also volunteered to do live gigs. On Sunday 10th May the activist group LGBT Noise organised a *Rally For Marriage* which attracted nearly 5,000 people to Dublin's Merrion Square. Mundy, The Nualas and the gay and lesbian choir Gloria performed at the event. Each of those who attended held up a banner saying 'equal', creating some of the most visually influential images of the campaign.

Coming up to the last weekend, the volume and momentum of the Yes Equality campaign seemed to be increasing exponentially. The question on everybody's minds, however, was whether or not all this activity was helping the Yes vote in the polls.

CHAPTER 9

Closing Argument

15th MAY TO 22nd MAY 2015

Friday 15th of May was the most nerve-racking day of the campaign. The *Irish Times* was due to publish an IPSOS/MRBI poll on the referendum the following morning. Then the *Sunday Business Post* would have a poll from Red C, the *Sunday Independent* would have one from Millward Brown, and the *Sunday Times* would publish one from Behaviour and Attitudes. After two weeks without any published polls, four were coming along together. They would be the last polls of the campaign.

There was a poignant and pleasant surprise for the campaign in the *Irish Times* that morning in the form of Ursula Halligan's powerful and moving piece in which she came out as a lesbian in support of the Yes campaign.

Early in the afternoon the campaign also received other important news. Kathleen Hunt had been keeping in close contact with the Franchise Section in the Department of the Environment, where she sought details of how many people had applied to get on the supplementary register for the referendum. They had finally finished compiling the figures and they were beyond even Yes Equality's expectations. In all, 65,911 people had been added to the register, a record number for any referendum, and an early indicator that turnout was going to be high. The communications team issued an immediate statement in Brian's name welcoming the fact that so many had gone to the trouble of making sure they could vote on this important constitutional change.

Staff in Clarendon Street were also busy making plans for a National Canvass Day that would kick off at 11 a.m. that Saturday at key points in all cities and at as many major towns as possible. Sandra, Patrick and the distribution team were co-ordinating forty-five different literature drops to different groups around the country for the weekend.

Even though minds were focused on the task and on putting in place preparations to launch a major Get Out The Vote effort, everyone in Yes Equality was nervous about what the weekend of polls would hold.

Although privately they were confident, Brian, Gráinne and Noel met to plan what the campaign's response should be if the news in the polls was not good. If that happened, then it would be important not only to maintain morale but also to keep supporters and spokespersons calm and measured, to avoid any sense of panic, any negativity or any nasty reactions.

On Friday morning Noel had picked up intelligence that the numbers in the RED C poll still looked good for Yes. He shared this only with Brian and Gráinne.

At about 5.30 p.m. Brian decided he could wait no longer and rang a contact in the *Irish Times* who might know something about their poll. Brian didn't pressurise them for the precise numbers, but just asked whether the Yes campaign had anything to worry about. 'Nothing at all,' was the reply he got. Brian told Gráinne and Noel. It was all they needed to hear. Together with the indications on the Red C poll it confirmed there was going to be no poll wobble. They decided, in fairness to Brian's contact, not to tell anyone else yet. The poll figures would be up online at midnight and probably on Twitter shortly before that. As they returned to their desks, however, they couldn't resist a private exchange of smiles. Their judgement on the strategy had been correct. Now it was steady as she goes to polling day.

On his way to take the Luas home that evening, Noel happened on Fergus Finlay, who was canvassing the Stephen's Green stop with Tánaiste Joan Burton and a Labour Party crew. 'Me stomach has been in knots for two days. Is there any news on the polls?' Fergus begged. Noel reassured him that the word they had was that all would be ok. Over the next few hours, however, several in the campaign got panicked texts and phone calls from journalists and politicians as a rumour had swept through RTÉ that the *Irish Times* poll was showing a collapse in the Yes Vote. It simply wasn't true. The *Irish Times* front page led the next morning with an extraordinary graphic showing 70 per cent Yes and 30 per cent No. Those were the poll figures when Don't Knows were excluded; nobody believed the Yes vote would actually be that high, but the key point was that it was holding up.

A conference call with the Advisory Group had been arranged for 10 a.m. on the Saturday morning in case the polling required any strategy adjustment. It didn't. All were obviously happy; it was agreed that the priority now was to avoid complacency and focus on turnout. They had seen the full details of the *Irish Times* poll at that stage, so Noel and Brian were able to confirm that support for Yes was holding up in all age-groups and all socio-economic demographics at the same level as a month earlier. The only surprisingly low figure was among Fianna Fáil voters and voters in Munster. Tiernan reached out to Fianna Fáil leader Mícheál Martin and encouraged him towards high-profile contributions on Monday or Tuesday. In fairness, Fianna Fáil had already complained to RTÉ that their leader couldn't get a look in. The following Monday Martin did very well in a debate with John Waters on Vincent Browne's TV3 programme. He also did well in a head to head against Bruce Arnold on the RTÉ *Morning Ireland* radio news programme on Tuesday.

On Saturday morning itself, however, the National Canvass was the key event. More than 400 people gathered outside the GPO for the Dublin kick-off. Earlier in the week Justin McAleese had come up with the idea of a photo call at the launch entitled 'Fathers for Yes' featuring his own dad Martin, Ashok Varadkar and Tom Curran. It worked beyond his wildest expectations. The picture of the three of them against a backdrop of the GPO decorated with hundreds of Yes canvassers was carried by several media outlets.

For Gráinne, this was to be the most poignant and memorable moment of the campaign. Watching these three quiet and dignified men standing up for their gay sons in front of the site of the birth of the Republic was astounding, especially as they were surrounded by an enthusiastic crew of Yes Equality canvassers, representative of the thousands mobilised for the cause throughout the country that weekend.

After the photo call, Brian led half the volunteers south of the River Liffey to Grafton Street, while Gráinne took the other half round the corner to Henry Street. On both sides of the city the reaction to canvassers was equally positive; almost everyone they met wanted to take literature and they met hundreds wearing or asking for YES or TÁ badges. These scenes were repeated throughout Ireland as volunteers from political parties and local Yes Equality groups joined up to launch canvasses at seventy different points across the country. In Mayo the national canvass began from seventeen different points in the county. In Cork they had 279 volunteers out that day.

News of the other polls filtered out on Saturday evening. RED C had the Yes vote at 69 per cent, Behaviour and Attitudes had it at 63 per cent. The *Sunday Independent* Millward Browne poll had Yes at 53 per cent and No at 23 per cent before Don't Knows were excluded. They put a peculiar headline on their front page claiming 'Yes Vote in Free Fall'. It was nonsense, not even supported by the findings of their own poll. Yes Equality leaders and politicians could see that, but the claim did confuse and concern those less experienced in how newspapers sometime play with poll figures for more dramatic headlines. The task was to strike a balance between reassurance and complacency and to focus all efforts on getting out the vote. As Noel put it in a tweet on Sunday morning: 'The bottom line is four polls show the Yes over the No at two to one, now it's all about turnout.'

A calm set in over Yes Equality headquarters, helped by the careful planning of that last week of the campaign. When they had originally developed their one-page plan in mid-March, the trio had envisaged a final closing argument phase of the campaign. All through April and early May staffers repeatedly asked the three of them what that closing argument would be. 'We don't know,' they used to reply. 'We will only know it when the time comes.'

The most important things they had learned during the previous two months were that the new positive style of campaigning worked, and that it was personal appeals and personal stories which had the greatest impact on voters. The closing argument would have to reflect that. The decision was made to focus the last phase of messaging on how the gay men and lesbian women seeking equality were part of every voter's community.

That this should be the closing argument was crystallised for everyone in headquarters when the creative staff in Havas emailed in some roughs of a poster and advertising idea they had come up with. It depicted a person holding a large card saying, 'I am your brother, your teacher, your friend. Vote Yes for me.' It was perfect and they decided to produce different versions of the poster involving six different people.

The challenge now, however, was to get it produced in time. There was a saying in headquarters during the month of May that if an idea couldn't be implemented in forty-eight hours, then it was of no use. This idea had to be implemented in twenty-four. Odhrán Allen, who was mental health policy officer with GLEN, took the lead in sourcing five other gay or lesbian people of different ages for a photo shoot by the photographer Cáit Fahey. It took place the following evening in the back garden of the home of Peter O'Dwyer, Creative Director of Havas. The atmosphere as they posed was jovial but poignant; each of them was putting themselves out in the public space by making a personal appeal for their equality to be recognised, albeit at a time when it seemed Ireland was likely to say Yes. Twelve hours later the posters were printed.

There was only time to get a sprinkling of them up in Dublin, but a media photo call was arranged for Grafton Street on the Friday afternoon, featuring the people pictured in the posters, each holding their own poster in front of them. It got widespread coverage in the daily and Sunday newspapers and also online.

The success of the ongoing fundraising effort meant that there was also a budget for an intensive newspaper advertising campaign over the last week. It was decided that rather than rebutting No arguments, these adverts should also feature the photos, along with positive appeals directly from gay and lesbian people. The media-buying project was overseen by Orla Howard, whose industry savvy and robust use of bulk-buying power meant they managed to book quarter-page ads in all Sunday and daily nationals and most of the regionals at a very competitive rate. The picture adverts with their positive appeals contrasted sharply with the negative, text-laden and somewhat scary half-page adverts that Mothers and Fathers Matter bought in many of the same papers.

The 'real people' theme was also developed in one of the final press conferences of the campaign, which launched a video *The Kids Are Alright,* featuring adult children of gay and lesbian couples, including Evan Barry, speaking about their upbringing and reassuring voters that their parents had done a great job. Caroline O'Sullivan of the ISPCC and Tanya Ward of the Children's Rights Alliance also appeared on the panel for this event to emphasise one last time how frontline children's organisations were supporting marriage equality.

This last week of Yes Equality's effort throughout the country was focused on a Get Out the Vote (GOTV) operation of a type never previously seen in an Irish referendum. Brian led this effort. Three aspects arising from the underlying analysis of poll data shaped his strategy. First, a higher turnout would increase the chances of a Yes victory and the size of any win. Secondly, support for the referendum was overwhelming among younger and more technologically literate voters. Thirdly, the principled reason given by most electors for why they had not voted in previous referendums was that it hadn't been convenient on the day. If voters could be encouraged to consider how they were likely to spend Friday 22nd May and to make a plan for voting within it, then they were more likely to actually get to a polling station.

The campaign had been wary of an over-concentration on social media, but now the strategy was to use social media to drive turnout. The GOTV project included a new website: getmetothevoteontime. ie, where voters were invited to register their mobile number and indicate the time when they were most likely to vote. If they did so, they got a text reminding them to vote twenty-four hours before, and also an hour before, their selected voting time. Some 2,900 people signed up for the website but the surrounding publicity also focused minds on the precise arrangements for getting to a polling station on Friday. The actress Saoirse Ronan, herself a first-time voter, did a special photo call at Clerys clock on Dublin's O'Connell Street to promote this initiative on Sunday 17th May. Her message was targeted at other younger voters: 'This is something that will change our futures and define our generation. If we don't vote, it's on us' she said.

Partner organisations were also involved in GOTV efforts. At the last mobilisation meeting at Clarendon Street, the student unions set out plans to camp outside polling stations before polls opened. The hope was that these well-planned 'spontaneous' queues would become a talking point on social media and create hype on polling day. Odhrán Allen set about organising similar early voting events in other parts of the country.

Yes Equality itself made and posted voter education videos and several infographics showing first-time voters how to vote and reminding all voters to bring identification and not to wear Yes Equality t-shirts or badges to the polling station. The campaign also had voting day stickers with the slogan 'I've Voted. Have You?', which proved extremely popular.

Meanwhile, as expected, the social media conversations on the referendum reached fever pitch in the final days of the campaign and not just in Ireland. There were nearly one billion global impressions for #marref generated from 467,323 Twitter mentions by 384,002 users in this final week, across every corner of the globe, in particular from countries with a strong Irish heritage. Yes Equality's small social media team at headquarters and its legions of online activists helped to drive this intense social media activity.

While all this was going on, there were also a number of high-profile broadcast media outings to be addressed. Gráinne was to do a Newstalk debate on the *George Hook Show* live from Limerick on the Monday before polling. That same evening Minister Alex White and Colm O'Gorman were to represent the Yes side on the Today FM debate on Matt Cooper's radio programme. Most importantly of all, Alex, Colm and Senator Katherine Zappone were to participate in the last televised debate on *Prime Time* on Tuesday night.

To the dismay of Yes Equality, the *Claire Byrne Show* was also returning to the topic of the referendum and surrogacy for a segment of its programme on Monday night. They planned two eight-minute interviews, one with Health Minister Leo Varadkar and another with a No campaigner. On the Monday evening Noel was asked to join the Minister and some of his advisors for a prep session. Varadkar had some important information that could help to put the surrogacy issues in context. He explained on the programme that there were 300,000 couples in Ireland who had fertility difficulties. There were only about ten to twelve children born each year in Ireland through surrogacy, almost all of them to an opposite-sex couple. He pointed out that anonymous sperm or egg donations had already been banned in Ireland. The Minister went on to confirm that forthcoming legislation would not only ban all commercial surrogacy but would require those seeking to avail of altruistic surrogacy to be approved in advance on criteria similar to that currently operating for adoption. This again was an important reassurance for those with concerns about surrogacy, irrespective of whether they believed it would be affected by the referendum.

That same night, Kieran Rose had done a head-to-head debate on UTV Ireland with Senator Ronan Mullen which had also gone well for the Yes side. Kieran's understated tone contrasted with the increasingly argumentative approach Senator Mullen was adopting. Kieran's key contributions to the campaign in various interviews was to set the referendum in the context of the thirty years'

struggle for gay and lesbian equality which he and others had em-
barked upon decades earlier.

Those participating in the other debates had gathered for
a joint session on Sunday evening. Noel's message to them was
blunt – all the indicators were that the referendum was won, the
objective was to hold what they had and not to spook the voters:
'You don't have to win the debates; just don't mess up.' There was
a pressing need, Brian told them, to calm things down in the
public debate and let the electorate have the space to reflect before
polling day. Above all else, Cathy warned them not to be provoked
into attacking the other side. Noel read them a prescient point
that Thalia Zepatos, who had been following the campaign on
line from Washington, had made in an email the previous day:
'It seems to me that if it's possible to lower the intensity of the
debate in the closing days, that would be helpful. One thing we
know from our research here is that conflicted voters are trying to
figure out which side they feel more comfortable with, so we have
to come across as reasonable, solid, non-threatening, etc. I know
how hard this must be in the context of the final debates and the
misdirection of the opposition, but our research shows that they
gain points by showing us as "pushy" and themselves as "victims".
So if there's any way to calm people down and remind them that
this is about their friends and neighbours, etc. etc., I think that
would be very helpful in the closing days.'

This chimed with what everyone in Yes Equality and in the
political parties in Ireland believed. At that moment, it was not
about winning any arguments. The voters had resolved the issues
in their own minds. It was all about calm, respectful debate in the
last days.

The outing on George Hook's programme from Limerick on
Monday evening was the one Gráinne enjoyed the most. The six-hour
round trip was almost a welcome break from the office, and Mark
Dempsey had kindly volunteered to do the driving. The Newstalk
debate was more good-natured than others. George Hook was firm
but respectful to all participants. The No speakers included Patrick

Treacy SC, a relatively new voice on the No side, whose tone was always polite, affable and thus all the more effective. Amongst his most clever arguments was the last-minute suggestion that people should vote down the referendum and the government should come back with a new proposal to put civil partnership in the Constitution. Gráinne told listeners that gay and lesbian couples should not be asked to settle for second best. They deserved equality and the right to marriage like everyone else; now was the time to share it with them. Treacy would go on to make the same argument on *Claire Byrne Live* that night and the following night on *Prime Time*.

The Today FM debate was a much more rowdy affair. The No speakers were Breda O'Brien and Senator Jim Walsh, who some weeks earlier had resigned the Fianna Fáil party whip to vote against the Children and Family Relationships Bill. They were among the more provocative No spokespersons and at times the debate descended into a shouting match. On occasion it might have seemed to uninitiated listeners that O'Gorman and White were ganging up on O'Brien, who once again came across as a mild-mannered teacher calmly trying to express reservations. Listening in Clarendon Street, some feared it might bode ill for the *Prime Time* debate the following night, which was more important because it was on TV and had a much larger audience.

They need not have worried. This last debate was more measured. It was well chaired by Miriam O'Callaghan and, although it got tetchy in the second half, in part because all participants were tiring, the Yes side kept their cool. As it happened, the most robust participant was Senator Ronan Mullen, whose outrage at one stage in the debate forced his voice to a very high pitch. Senator Katherine Zappone was passionate and persuasive, Colm was typically effective and showed admirable restraint and Alex White made key interventions, dealing calmly and ably with all the controversial issues.

In Clarendon Street, everyone breathed a sigh of relief that the Yes side had survived the last debates. There were now only two and a half days to go before the broadcast moratorium on reporting the campaign would take effect. However, before that happened, the

Yes campaign would field the most impressive advocate yet for the marriage equality cause.

It had always been intended that Mary McAleese would make a carefully timed intervention in the campaign. The former President, who is also a constitutional lawyer and canon lawyer, had been identified as a most important voice. The strategic decisions were around where and in what forum she should speak, and, most importantly, when she would do so.

McAleese was a visiting lecturer at the University of Notre Dame in Indiana that spring and did not return to Ireland until mid-May. She had expressed her strong views in favour of the referendum in an interview with George Hook, who had done a special broadcast for Newstalk radio from Notre Dame in early April. While this got some coverage, it had been limited, and by the last few days its impact had faded. A more substantial McAleese intervention was still required.

In the wake of the George Hook interview, Mary's son Justin, who was one of the Yes Equality campaign members in the Dublin Bay South constituency, had written a moving piece for the *Irish Independent* about growing up gay in Ireland. He made a passionate appeal for a Yes vote so that Ireland could be a country that allows people to 'express their sexuality and allows them to express their love in the same way as their straight brothers and sisters'.

Mary McAleese had been a long-time supporter of the work of BeLonG To and, working with her former adviser Maura Grant, had decided to do her referendum event with them. That made sense to everyone. The event was originally scheduled for Thursday 14th May, but as the campaign developed, the former president sent word through Justin, enquiring as to whether BeLonG To and Yes Equality thought it might be best left until even later. It was decided to move it back to the Tuesday before polling day, the 19th, partly so that she could reply to any issues which flowed from the last round of debates and, more importantly, so that her solid argument and reassuring voice was among the last that voters heard.

While in Notre Dame she had been thinking about what she would say, but as soon as she got back to Dublin she wanted to get an up-to-date sense of the campaign. Over coffee and croissants in Justin's apartment shortly after she landed, Noel and Justin took her and her husband Martin, through the various twists and turns of the argument over the previous weeks. The former president needed little guidance, having been absorbed in the issue of gay and lesbian equality for decades and also having a strong instinctive feel for how best to articulate her views to voters. The only thing Noel asked of her on behalf of Yes Equality was that she would make herself available for extended one-on-one interviews with all the main media outlets after her speech. McAleese readily agreed.

The arrangements were left in the competent hands of Michael Barron and his team at BeLonG To with McAleese's former press officer Gráinne Mooney and Cathy Madden helping out with the press arrangements.

The McAleese event was held at 10 a.m. in the Wood Quay Centre in Dublin. The audience included many of the gay and lesbian young people whom BeLong To worked with, their families, and invited guests from other groups involved in the campaign. Michel Barron introduced her and the former President gave a forty-minute exposition of the reason why marriage equality was now an imperative. She also systematically deconstructed the various arguments advanced by the Catholic Church and others who opposed it. She told of her own involvement in the campaign for homosexual law reform as a young academic in Trinity College Dublin and then spoke of her hopes and fears as the mother of a gay son. 'We who are parents, brothers and sisters, colleagues and friends of Ireland's gay citizens know how they have suffered because of second-class citizenship,' she said. 'This referendum is about them and them alone,' she added. 'The only children affected by this referendum will be Ireland's gay children. It is their future which is at stake. It is in our hands. We, the majority, have to make it happen for them and for all the unborn gay children who are relying on us to end the branding, end the isolation, end the inequality, literally once and for all.'

To those who claimed that marriage equality would undermine marriage, she said, 'A Yes vote costs the rest of us nothing. A No vote costs our gay children everything.' She was strongly critical both of the Church teaching on homosexuality, and of their guidance on this referendum; she tackled the issue of surrogacy head on. 'No one in Ireland, whether heterosexual or homosexual, has a legal or constitutional right to procreation using surrogacy. This referendum, if passed, will certainly not create any such right. It is a nonsense to think it could.' Her principal argument was focused, however, on how a Yes vote on Friday would end the 'branding and exclusion' which gay and lesbians in Ireland felt, and would help to dismantle what she called 'the architecture of homophobia'.

She then stood in an adjoining room for almost two hours talking to the media one on one. She did a live interview on the telephone with the *Pat Kenny Show* on Newstalk, and recorded a piece for RTE radio's *News at One*, and she talked to correspondents from all the national print media. The speech and the media engagement were immeasurably valuable to the campaign in those crucial final days and attracted saturation coverage. She had done everything the Yes Campaign needed to close the deal with voters and more.

That evening, the Taoiseach, Enda Kenny, did a live interview in studio with Bryan Dobson on the RTÉ *Six One News*. His message too was one of solid reassurance. He said that, as a Catholic, he had no issue about extending marriage rights to gay couples and that the electorate had nothing to fear by voting Yes.

The Taoiseach was followed by a live interview with the Archbishop of Dublin, Diarmuid Martin, who had agreed to make the closing argument for the No side. The Archbishop's interventions into the campaign over the previous weeks were curious and worrying for the Yes campaign. While other bishops had influence at most among practising Catholics, Diarmuid Martin had a higher profile and wider appeal because of his handling of the clerical abuse controversies and his prominence on various social justice issues. He seemed to have been bullied into publicly speaking out against the referendum by comments in the Catholic press suggesting that, by his silence, he was giving solace to the Yes side. In his various interviews he spoke about his reluctance to intervene, which in some ways made his intervention all the more effective. He talked on the *Six One* interview about how people needed to reflect on the importance of marriage and the big step they were being asked to take in redefining it. One line in his interview caused particular annoyance to the Yes campaign: 'If a couple get married in a Catholic ceremony that's a civil marriage.' This was inaccurate since the civil function performed by a priest in solemnising a marriage for the State is separate from the Catholic ceremony. It was seen as another example of the bishops deliberately confusing civil and sacramental marriage so as to imply that the referendum would have an impact on the Catholic ceremony. However, the campaign decided to let it ride and to simply issue a statement expressing disappointment.

As voting drew near, politicians and leading activists came in increasing numbers to Clarendon Street to wish the campaign well. At times the numbers were overwhelming and Brian and Gráinne struggled to do their day job while hosting the visitors, but the visits showed how central the Yes Equality HQ had become. Among those who dropped in during these last days were Simon Coveney TD, Leo Varadkar TD, Alan Shatter TD and Joan Collins TD. On one such visit Alex White TD, Labour Director of Elections, was overcome with emotion as he addressed the team. Joan Burton TD arrived bearing cupcakes along with John Lyons TD and his mother Josie, who was quick to tell Séamus Dooley, 'make yourself useful and make Joan a cup of tea – she's the Tánaiste!' Josie and the Tánaiste stood beside the tiny kitchen exchanging campaign stories with the team.

On Wednesday the campaign arranged a special photocall on Grafton Street at which Brian and Gráinne would present the 500,000th Yes Equality badge to a passer-by. For Brian this was the most poignant moment of the campaign. The badges had started as a gimmick for the Register to Vote effort the previous November but had become iconic markers of a personal commitment to equality, worn proudly by hundreds of thousands of people. Headquaters staff couldn't keep their pockets filled with them. Campaigners were constantly asked for them in the street. 'Would you have a spare TÁ badge?' became a refrain often heard. The Stephen's Green shop was selling them at €2 each or ten for a fiver, or fifty for a tenner. Bags and bags of badges had been distributed across the country to the Yes Equality groups. Fathers were coming in buying handfuls for family gatherings. One couple bought one for every guest at their wedding.

That day on Grafton Street Brian spoke to an older man who was ambling past them. 'Would you care for a Yes badge?' he asked. 'I'd be delighted,' replied the man. Seizing the opportunity, Brian asked him if he would be prepared to be photographed as the recipient of the 500,000th badge. 'I'd be very honoured to accept,' he replied. With twinkling eyes, eighty-five-year-old Vivian Sheehan (no relation), a native of Castletownbere, who had lived in Windy Arbour in Dundrum for decades, pulled his coat together, fixed his collar and with a big broad smile stood beside Gráinne as Brian pinned on the TÁ badge. It was the first moment Brian had allowed himself to feel the magic of the campaign, which he had ignored for the last few weeks in case it brought bad luck. 'If this charming, gentle, man is with us, how can we lose?' he thought.

On the Thursday, the eve of the poll, Yes Equality did one last event for the press photographers. Arrangements were made to transport the eight-foot-high wooden YES, which had been made for local events in Cavan, to Dublin. All the personalities and organisations involved in the wider Yes campaign were invited to come and give 'one last push for Yes' in front of the cameras. The event was held at the bottom of Clarendon Street, just down from the Gaiety Theatre. The Tánaiste Joan Burton was among those who came along. Taoiseach Enda Kenny happened on the photo call on his way to a business launch nearby and was also included. It was a chaotic but light-hearted event, with an atmosphere that risked tipping over from confidence to giddiness. Cathy and Andrew had instructed the team to look and act serious, but the photographers persuaded Craig Dwyer to climb up on top of the wooden structure amid cheers which were quickly silenced. There were to be no premature signs of celebration.

Otherwise, Thursday was a surreal day in the Clarendon Street HQ, and indeed for most campaigners throughout the country.

Fatigue was beginning to set in. Everyone was running on reserves of adrenaline. Most felt that if polling data and canvass returns were anywhere near accurate, the referendum was probably won, but that confidence sat side by side with a growing sense of the significance which the result would have and how many were dependent on a positive outcome.

There was still much work to be done. A high-visibility operation was being put in place along the two canals and at other key junctions across Dublin. Similar exercises were being put in place in prime locations in other towns and cities, including Cork, where they were also doing a special eve of poll leaflet drop.

Brian and Gráinne had also quietly begun making preparations for the day of the count. They were conscious that it would be important for them, as leaders of the campaign and leaders in the gay and lesbian community, to channel and reflect what a victory in this referendum would mean. They had asked Donal Cronin to work on remarks that might be made on Saturday when the result was announced. When presented with the first draft on Thursday morning, they were impressed, but had additional thoughts on how best to capture the significance of the outcome. Between then and the middle of Friday afternoon, drafts of the speech travelled between the three of them on emails with the subject line 'Remarks welcoming a Yes vote – just in case'.

Of course they should also have been preparing a version to use if the referendum was lost, but they just couldn't bring themselves to do it, not because of any over-confidence, but because at this stage, when victory meant so much, losing was just unconscionable; it would be devastating. Brian, Gráinne, Noel and Mark had been asked to write pieces for a special commemorative edition of *Gay Community News* which was to be published the week after the referendum. Separately they each decided once again that they could only write this premised on a Yes victory.

They also had Adam May work with Andrew and Craig on graphics and messaging which would go up on the Yes Equality website when the result was announced, assuming it was positive. They also asked him to develop designs for 'Thank You' advertisements to be placed in the newspapers on Sunday and Monday. In part this activity was filling time and burning up nervous energy, but on another level it was typical of the attention to detail and emphasis on preparedness that had been a hallmark of Bráinne's leadership throughout the campaign.

On Thursday evening the mobilisation side of the office was busy with last-minute preparations for polling day, but the communications operation was quiet. The last press releases had been issued and, apart from some polling day messaging on social media, there was little to be done.

Over the next couple of hours, however, the team in Clarendon Street, like many in the country generally, were to be floored by a phenomenal development online.

It started as a trickle in the late afternoon. Occasional posts started appearing on Twitter from Irish people saying how they were setting off to the airport to catch a plane to Ireland and they began using the hashtag #hometovote. It grew into a tidal wave of tweets as thousands of people from as far away as Canada, Australia, Africa and Asia shared photos and messages charting their return journey. The impact of all these individual trips home to Ireland being documented live on social media was incredible. The viral effect was boosted further as those at home, or others abroad who were not travelling home, spotted the phenomenon and tweeted on the #hometovote hashtag about how moved they were by what was occurring. It touched people partly because of the pain of Irish emigration and its unhappy recurrence in recent years, but also because it said something about the passion that fuelled the Yes campaign and the emotional investment that so many had in the outcome.

Over the previous weeks there had been some indications of the levels of support for the referendum among the Irish abroad. The #bemyyes campaign had seen hundreds of videos and thousands of messages posted by emigrants encouraging voters back in Ireland to vote Yes on their behalf. In places like New York, Sydney and

Brussels, Irish emigrants had gathered for group photographs, which they then posted online to make the same point.

Nobody had expected, however, that so many emigrants would actually make plans to be at a polling station themselves in Ireland on referendum day. To watch them tell the story of how they were doing so, tweet-by-tweet, was inspirational and overwhelming.

In all, 72,000 individual messages using the #hometovote hashtag were posted between 5 p.m. on Thursday and 5 p.m. on Friday. They included pictures of the 9.10 p.m. Thursday train from London to Holyhead, where those returning to vote filled carriages and decorated them with rainbow balloons. It included pictures of the large queues on Thursday evening at immigration in Dublin airport. People took pictures of their Irish passports at check-in desks in airports all over the world or posted selfies from planes or trains that were bringing them home. One returnee posted a picture of his bedroom, which his mother had fitted out in rainbow curtains and a rainbow bedspread, to welcome him home from London to vote. Thousands poured into Dublin airport wearing Yes Equality badges or carrying home-made rainbow-coloured signs. The artist Annie West worked up a sketch of the crowds of Irish gathering to get through Dublin airport to vote, and when she posted it on Twitter it got more than 1,200 re-tweets in six hours. The impact of what was happening was summed up in a tweet by the comedian Colm O'Regan: 'The #hometovote is like when you are watching *The Hobbit* and the army of elves you've forgotten from earlier in the film arrive over the hill.' More than 4,100 people retweeted it.

If the #hometovote phenomena had happened in another era it would have given rise to no more than rumours or sporadic anecdotes, but in the age of social media everyone could watch it happen in real time online. In Clarendon Street they were moved and overjoyed; those coming home to vote were coming home to vote Yes, and their efforts to do so would surely motivate those still living in Ireland to do the same in very large numbers.

Polls opened at 7 a.m. on Friday 22nd May and immediately it was obvious that something truly historic was happening. There were queues outside several polling stations in Dublin, and not only at those where they had been planned. By mid-morning experienced presiding officers and polling clerks were telling of record numbers turning out, and saying that many of them were younger and more enthusiastic than in previous referendums. #ivoted was the leading trend on Twitter in Ireland from early morning and for most of the day #Voteyes was the top trend worldwide. The taxi company Hailo offered free trips to the polling stations. On the Google search home page the company posted a message: 'Google Supports Marriage Equality #proudtolove'. Facebook added an 'I've Voted' icon to Irish pages which acted as a further prompt to those who hadn't yet gone to vote. In Clarendon Street, polling day came with an eerie ease to the relentless emails, meetings and phone calls. The campaign team trickled in a bit later than usual having taken the time to cast their votes in their local polling stations.

Noel voted with his wife Sinéad in Beechwood in Ranelagh and found the place very busy just after 8 a.m. Their six-year-old son, Seamus, whom they always brought along to the polling station, insisted they 'vote Yes Equality' before bringing him to school. When they explained to him that there was also another referendum to reduce the age at which people could be elected president, he wanted to know why there wasn't a referendum to reduce the voting age to six. Andrew voted in Rathgar with his pal Ronan Healy, both of them in disbelief that the day had arrived at last. Tiernan, having spent the last weekend canvassing in his native Bundoran, arranged with three gay friends to vote together at their local Inchicore polling station at 7am. He knew one of the ladies officiating at the desk from the local community and she gave them a warm smile. It was wonderful, he remarked to his pals, to vote for yourself, even though you are not on the ballot paper. Sandra and her partner Marion also voted early in Crumlin. Moninne with Clodagh and their daughter Edie went with Denise and Paula and their sons Benán and Cian to the polling station in Dalkey.

Gráinne and Patricia were accompanied for their trip to vote in Glasnevin by the political colour writer Lisa Hand and a photographer from the *Irish Independent*. Brian's local polling station was in Beggars Bush, where his voting was captured by Peter Morrison of Associated Press for the *New York Times*. All knew from the numbers and age profile of those voting, and the atmosphere in the polling stations, that the turnout was of a size and composition that suggested a decisive Yes victory.

Any notion that the headquarters staff had that their work was done was quickly dispelled when Brian called the team to the first of three 'state of the nation's voting' meetings held over the course of that day. He and the social media team had a whole set of messages to broadcast, depending on turnout across the nation. The alerts sent urgent ripples through the Yes Equality network as each Yes Equality group in turn relayed the rallying calls to their volunteers. Even on polling day itself nothing was left to chance, no eventuality unconsidered, no avenue unexplored.

Brian and Gráinne did a couple of video blogs on social media in one last effort to encourage people to vote. As the warm sunny evening approached, a carnival atmosphere broke out among activists in some areas. The Yes Bus, which was touring the capital, was stopped regularly by people who wanted to pose for photographs with it. Mark Kelly, Pia Jenning and Grace Mulvey drove around Dublin in the ICCL's 'voter motor', encouraging people to vote and posting pictures online of the spontaneous rainbow scenes that they came across. Volunteers involved in the visibility effort aimed at homeward-bound traffic in cities and towns all over the country reported thousands of cars honking their horns in support, some of them with rainbow flags swinging out their windows. Yes Equality Ballina, like many groups, had arranged to stand at main junctions that evening, with hand-made signs saying 'Honk if You're Voting Yes'. At one point they rang Sandra and relayed the noisy traffic response down the line. She quickly put them on speakerphone so everyone in the office could hear. Charlie Flanagan TD, Foreign Affairs Minister, rang from Kilkenny to tell them about the youthful positive energy of the atmosphere at polling stations and key junctions in the city as the sun was setting. Una Mullally was the first of many on Twitter to describe the atmosphere in Dublin as something akin to a 'Gay Italia 90'.

Brian and Gráinne did a wrap up and thank you session with all the Clarendon Street staff just after 5.30 p.m., but most still stayed on in the office after that. About half an hour later, Yvonne Judge, who was monitoring online activity to the very end, called them all over to her computer screen. 'You have to see this,' she said. The latest clip to go viral on the #hometovote hashtag was a video posted a short time earlier of Oonagh Murphy, one of those behind the Get The Boat 2 Vote initiative, leading a group of Irish emigrants from London singing the haunting ballad 'She Moves Through the Fair' as their ferry sailed into Dublin. The video was just over a minute long and the lyrics included the line 'It will not be long now, 'til our wedding day.' In Clarendon Street they watched it first in silence and then in sobs; the combination of emotion and exhaustion had got too much.

Over the next few hours each of them left the office, ending their last campaign day. All over the country Yes Equality campaigners were doing the same as the polling stations closed. Like an army standing down, they each retreated to their private space in the hope of getting whatever sleep would come before morning and the opening of the ballot boxes.

CHAPTER 10

An Extraordinary Day

23rd MAY 2015

Saturday 23rd May was a beautiful morning in Dublin, and throughout most of Ireland as Yes campaigners rose early and hopefully.

Gráinne, who had been awake since sunrise, sat up in bed at about 6 a.m. It felt like the first day of the Leaving Cert all over again – she had done all she could, the day had arrived and the best thing was that it would be over by sunset. She felt sick with anxiety.

She had agreed to go on radio for the *Morning Ireland* Referendum Special and dressed quietly, putting on a pair of new navy shoes to accompany the navy dress that she had chosen as appropriate for the day ahead, an understated but classic look, in keeping with the spokesperson role she had constructed and delivered during the campaign. A short time later she took a quiet taxi ride over to RTÉ in Montrose with Cathy Madden.

Brian, who had also been awake at an ungodly hour, put on one of his sharp blue suits and was in Clarendon Street by 8.30 a.m., going through wrap-up arrangements with Kathleen Hunt while waiting for the first tally information from around the country. The previous day, Yes Equality had set up a WhatsApp group with tally leaders for each count centre and had asked them to post any useful information they had as soon as possible after 9 a.m.

Noel, as a regular political pundit, was due to be in RTÉ for the start of their television coverage at 10 a.m., although, as a campaigner, it would be a count day with a difference this time, even for him. Before going to RTÉ he planned to begin the day where he always liked to, at the Dublin count centre in the RDS as the ballot boxes were opened. When he arrived at 8.30 a.m., he was struck, not for the first time in this campaign, by the size and composition of the crowd who had gathered. He had seen large numbers at general election counts over the years, but had never seen anything like this for a referendum. As they waited to get into the count centre, veteran politicos were giving hurried lessons in tally techniques to hundreds of first-time Yes Equality campaigners.

Just before the doors of the RDS opened, Tiernan Brady spoke to one group, reinforcing one last time the positive message of respect that he and others had shaped for the campaign: 'When you are in here today, you will be the face to the world of what is happening in this count centre. There will be people from all over the world here and there will be people who don't agree with us here. We have to remember the respect and dignity that we brought to this campaign and we will make sure that on the last day of this campaign, respect and dignity will be as real in this room as we made it in every single corner of our capital city.'

At 9 a.m. sharp in the RDS and at the other count centres throughout the country the seals on the ballots boxes were broken and thousands of ballot papers were tossed out onto the tables. As the ballot papers began to be sorted, everyone could see that something incredible was happening. The previous day the Irish people had become the first in the world to be asked whether they would put marriage equality into their Constitution. It was immediately clear that their answer was Yes; a resounding, definitive, equality-loving Yes.

Noel leaned over the shoulders of dozens of tally people monitoring papers from polling stations all over the city and saw that the Yes majority held steady across all areas, irrespective of their socio-economic make-up or previous patterns of political support.

Meanwhile, Gráinne and Cathy were in the anteroom of the *Morning Ireland* studio. Sitting beside them was John Murray, Chair of the Iona Institute, with whom they had exchanged a civil handshake on arrival. On air, RTÉ's political correspondent Martina Fitzgerald and Harry McGee of the *Irish Times*, called it for Yes at twelve minutes past nine. The political scientist David Farrell told listeners that the turnout could be the highest ever for a referendum. There had, he said, 'been a huge mobilisation of the younger voters and an amazing use of social media for the first time'.

On his way out of the studio McGee shook hands with Gráinne, saying he had had no doubt it was a Yes, and the only question remaining was by how much. Gráinne could finally let herself believe it. Her task, however, was to remain calm; there would be no victory cries or triumphalism; the tone for count day would remain quiet and respectful, as it had been throughout the campaign. The Fianna Fáil leader, Micheál Martin, put it well from the Cork count centre: 'The tone of the campaign was what won through,' he said, and 'that was largely down to the Yes Equality campaign'. The programme then went to an ad break and when she was brought into studio Gráinne was grabbed by the Labour TD John Lyons, who gave her a huge hug and insisted on a photo of the two of them in the studio together, tweeting it before the studio door closed behind her. It was the first of hundreds of hugs and selfies she and Brian were invited to participate in that day.

Meanwhile, Brian and the others in Clarendon Street watched the story unfold on the WhatsApp group. The victory would not be confined to Dublin. Noel Sharkey of Yes Equality Donegal South West posted at 9.15 a.m.: 'First box tally – Ballyshannon – 60 per cent Yes, 40 per cent No'. A few minutes later Vivian Cummins told them that in Kildare South the preliminary total was running 60/40 Yes. The Wicklow tallies were running at 65 per cent Yes. The Yes tally in Limerick City was running at 62 per cent and in Limerick County at 53 per cent Yes.

In the RDS and other count centres Yes Equality campaigners and their political colleagues also started to let themselves believe it was true. Weeks, months and years of pent-up emotion broke loose. Never had count centres seen so many tears, and all from the winning side.

The gay and lesbian people there tried to communicate what actually seeing the result confirmed on the ballot papers meant. It wasn't just about important constitutional change, it was also about being acknowledged as equals in their own country. During the campaign they had watched and listened to much antagonism from No speakers in the media debates, they had experienced homophobia on some doorsteps, they had feared that, silently, most Irish voters might share these intolerant views. Of course they hoped it was otherwise, but it was only when they saw X marked opposite YES on an overwhelming majority of the ballot papers that Saturday that they were finally reassured that their country saw them as equal.

Straight allies spoke of how they had got involved in Yes Equality out of family connections or friendship, or just because they wanted their country to be recognised as a hospitable place for those of all sexual orientations. They wanted to be a part of achieving real equality.

In the RDS, friends who had campaigned together embraced and hugged intensely. Couples kissed in celebration of the result and the new freedom to display public affection that it seemed to suggest. A posse of national and international photojournalists was on hand to capture the historic moment. A picture of an emotional Andrew Hyland, a key young leader of the marriage equality movement, embracing the veteran gay rights campaigner Senator David Norris was soon on *The Guardian* and *Belfast Telegraph* websites. A shot of Moninne and her partner Clodagh wrapped in a rainbow flag made its way onto the front page of the *Daily Mail* website and was reprinted in several newspapers the next day. A photo of Craig and his partner Paul Franey kissing among the celebrating crowd was on the front of the *New York Times* website. Similar scenes were repeated at count centres all across Ireland and featured in the following week's regional newspapers.

Those at the count centres listening to the radio coverage on earphones could hear *Morning Ireland* presenter Gavin Jennings describe Gráinne as having a very wide grin. He invited her to share her thoughts. She said, 'The national conversation driven by the seventy Yes Equality groups across Ireland looked like it was going our way. The people had not been directed how to vote,' she said. 'They had been approached by canvassers saying "I'm voting Yes, can I tell you why?".' She described how a high turn-out had always been Yes Equality's objective and spoke of her pride in this as 'the people's referendum'. She finished by saying: 'We began to get some sense of a possible win resulting from sharing our stories, stories about real lives with real impacts.' If the win that seemed to be emerging was real, it was, she said, 'Irish people telling us we belong. If the referendum carries, LGBT people will feel we fully belong.'

Noel was down the corridor on the panel in RTÉ's TV studio at 10 a.m. as the presenter, Bryan Dobson, did a series of live reports from correspondents in regional studios who had been speaking to contacts at count stations and were giving a feel for the outcome in their area. Noel suggested that they abandon the traditional ritual; he had more up-to-date and reliable information on his phone and he began to read out the WhatsApp postings from Yes Equality tally leaders to the television audience.

There was now no doubt that a decisive victory was on the cards. While RTÉ were still being cautious, emphasising that no actual results had been announced and these were just early tallies, Noel suggested that there was no longer any need for such caution: 'The question was binary,' he said. 'The tallies are reliable: it will be 70:30 in Dublin and will approach 2:1 Yes overall.'

After *Morning Ireland*, Gráinne and Cathy followed the coverage on their mobile phones between incoming messages from well-wishers. For Gráinne, one of the most poignant early calls was from a life-long friend, Fiona Casey, living in Nantes in France. Fiona was crying on the phone; she had listened and watched the coverage on francophone and English-speaking channels. 'So proud of you,' she said to Gráinne. 'It is amazing what you guys have done.' For a moment Gráinne lost her composure. The next call was from Senator Katherine Zappone who was at the City West count centre, where again the tallies were terrific. 'We have done it,' she called down the phone. 'I know,' Gráinne replied. 'Imagine, finally.' After a decade-long struggle they were now approaching certain victory. Gráinne next called Patricia, her partner, feeling the need to confirm what she was hearing on radio and TV. 'It's really happening, Trish,' she said. 'I know,' Patricia replied; 'just enjoy it now.'

Brian was due to be on the *Marian Finucane Show* at the top of her programme at 11 a.m. Just before he left Clarendon Street he took a call in the office from his mum. She was gathered with his sisters and their children in Kilrush and she said they were all glued to the TV, 'watching a better Ireland unfolding'. 'Your dad would have been very proud,' she said softly. The next call he took was from his ex-partner Ian Bathard, who'd been with him through much of the early struggle leading to this moment.

When he arrived at the studio in RTÉ, Brian was still wary of calling the scale of the result. He could scarcely believe it was going to be such a big win. It was way beyond anything he had imagined possible when they had started out in Clarendon Street 107 days before. On air he acknowledged the generosity of the Irish people and spoke of the powerful impact that the result would have on a young person, secretly LGBT, going to school on Monday morning to prepare for the Junior Cert exams. He or she could confidently know that they belonged in their own country. It had been worth the long struggle.

Coming up to 12 noon, Brian, Gráinne, Noel and Cathy met up for the first time that day in the RTÉ canteen, allowing themselves hugs of celebration and then taking a taxi to the count centre. As they approached the entrance to the RDS a line of well-wishers stood and applauded. Noel and Cathy stood back. Brian and Gráinne looked at each other; Brian took Gráinne's hand and they walked through the door into an assault of loud cheers, cameras and the familiar faces of HQ team members, Yes Equality campaigners, board members and friends.

In the doorway, Brian picked out the faces of Sandra and her partner Marion, and knowing what the result meant to them and their children, he was suddenly overcome with emotion. Gráinne had to hug and hold him for a moment while he regained his composure, and then they were separated and passed from embrace to embrace. The shouting and cheering continued as hundreds hugged them in turn to thank them.

The tallies from the Dublin South Bay constituency were almost complete; it was going to be a huge win there. Brian and Gráinne were pulled across the hall to where the boxes had been opened and were asked to stand up on a wooden bench and address the crowd. They delivered a short message of thanks to campaigners not just in Dublin Bay South but throughout the country.

Noel and Brian went back to RTÉ for other commitments. Brian was in studio on a panel with David Quinn, who had conceded on Twitter an hour earlier that the referendum would pass. They shook hands and David congratulated Brian on the result. Meanwhile Gráinne slipped off for a quiet celebratory lunch with Patricia, Moninne and Clodagh. The figures kept coming in. Dublin South Bay was going to be the best in the country, narrowly tipping Dublin South West and thereby depriving Darragh Genockey of the proceeds of his bet with Paddy Power. Ken Curtin rang with great news from Cork: all but ten ballot boxes in the county area contained a Yes majority.

The national result of the referendum was going to be announced at Dublin Castle around tea time, but already hundreds were gathering in the courtyard there to celebrate and wait for the official announcement. A stage for TV cameras had been set up at the top of the yard and a steady flow of politicians and campaigners began to appear on live links from lunchtime onwards. They included many who had played important roles in the win, such as Minister Frances Fitzgerald and Panti Bliss, Katherine Zappone and Ann Louise Gilligan, David Norris, Una Mullally and Colm O'Gorman.

Yes Equality had booked the large ballroom in the Ballsbridge Hotel for the day and invited the HQ team and Dublin activists to gather there with their families to watch the result. They hoped it would be a celebration, but until Saturday mid-morning, they couldn't be sure. Once the tally operation finished, the hotel became the gathering point for a large but strangely intimate and family-friendly celebration. Gathered in that room were many to whom the result mattered most.

Darina Brennan, head chef at the hotel, and a board member of Marriage Equality, had organised a room for Gráinne to freshen up in and to sleep in that night. Gráinne made her way there just before 2.30 p.m. but when the crowd outside spotted her taxi pulling in, shouts went up and there were bursts of spontaneous applause. Just at that moment the Yes Bus also arrived and for old times' sake Andy the driver blared out 'Happy' through the bus's speakers while Mary McDermott and the bus team did a victory dance.

When Brian arrived, he and Gráinne were ushered into the ballroom where by now about a thousand supporters, family and friends had gathered.

Word came from Justin McAleese that his parents too were on their way to be part of the celebrations. When Mary McAleese arrived, she was greeted with rapturous applause. Everyone stood, and stayed standing as she delivered a stunning four-minute impromptu speech which captured exactly what the day meant to all who had worked so hard on the result. 'The sun is splitting the stones outside,' she said. 'The place looks amazing, and I just feel we live in a wonderful country. Today we saw the Yes and the Tá in everybody's heart and it is wonderful.' Speaking of the impending result, she said: 'In or about an hour's time we will no longer need to say the phrase "gay marriage" in Ireland. We will just speak of marriage.'

In the late afternoon, Brian and Gráinne travelled with Noel and Cathy over to Dublin Castle. En route, Brian fielded calls from newspapers such as the *New York Times* who were looking for a response. It was that kind of day. As they made their way through the lower gates of the courtyard, the crowd parted for them and those close by broke into applause. When they got to the area at the top of the courtyard, it was like the backstage of a rock concert, only this time the celebrities were politicians and marriage equality campaigners, and the atmosphere, as well as being celebratory, was poignant. Fergus Finlay was there, full of emotion; Mark Kelly, Ailbhe Smyth and Kieran Rose savoured the result they had done so much to shape. There too was Eamon Gilmore, who had been so instrumental in making the referendum happen. Fergus boomed at Brian and Gráinne: 'Why are youse two not up on the bloody stage?' With that, Andrew grabbed Gráinne's hand, she grabbed Brian and next thing they knew they were on the raised camera platform with the crowd cheering for them as they had for other faces of the campaign all afternoon. The reality of what was taking place took hold. The crowd started shouting 'Bráinne, Bráinne, Bráinne!'

Brian's most memorable moments of that day were watching the joy others got from the result. In the last weeks of the campaign he had been getting an increasingly abusive and homophobic series of anonymous messages on his mobile; he had shrugged them off, and, thankfully, they were now drowned by a flood of congratulatory texts.

The official announcement of the overall national result took place a little while later in the Conference Centre in the bowels of Dublin Castle. The atmosphere among this smaller crowd, which was made up primarily of invited dignitaries and politicians, was more muted than that above ground but there was still some giddiness. 'It's wonderful isn't it?' beamed Pádraig MacLochlainn,TD, the Sinn Féin campaign director and a long-time supporter of the marriage equality cause. He was almost childlike in his excitement. Other politicians, such as Simon Coveney TD, Niall Collins TD, Frances Fitzgerald TD and Micheál Martin TD also showed their excitement. Taoiseach Enda Kenny and Tánaiste Joan Burton were justifiably happy at how decisive the result had been. Leo Varadkar was in a reflective mood: 'It's for days like this that we do politics, isn't it?' he said. Jerry Buttimer TD and Senator Katherine Zappone were simply beaming with happiness. The final result was 1,201,607 Yes votes to 734,300 No. All constituencies except Roscommon had Yes majorities and even there the No lead was only 1,029 votes. As the

official declaration ended, the crowd in the courtyard started to sing
'Amhrán na bhFiann', the national anthem.

When they went back up to the courtyard, Brian and Gráinne
were offered a microphone on the stage; they delivered some of
the opening lines of their prepared speech, but decided to save the
balance for their own event in the hotel later. The text was already
up on the Yes Equality web page under the banner headline 'Truly a
Nation of Equals'.

Then, as they made their way through the crowd, there were
more warm hugs, and this time also some warm champagne. If
the scenes inside Dublin Castle had been amazing, those they met
outside the gates were incredible. The crowd of thousands who
had gathered to be close to the result had spread out into a street
party. There were hundreds of rainbow flags, honking car horns
and toasts of celebration. People waved from windows overhead.
A political outcome was welcomed on the streets as never before.
They were hauled by hugs and handshakes down across Dame Street
through the Front Lounge pub and back up Parliament Street.

It was at this stage that Noel, who had held his composure
until then, was finally overcome, as dozens of people came up to
thank him for advocating in their cause during the campaign. He
had been in semi-shock all day, not at the result itself, but at how
much it meant to so many, and at what that said about the sting of
discrimination they had felt. He had given up the comfort of the
pundit's couch two months earlier because he felt he could make
a contribution to this campaign. Like so many straight people
who had got involved, he was now profoundly changed by the
experience. Dearbhail McDonald of the *Irish Independent*, who was
nearby, spotted and snapped Noel's teary Dame Street moment and
had it on Twitter in seconds.

Back on the stage in Ballsbridge, Bráinne delivered their crafted
and practised speech; it spoke of the values and the victory, and
they thanked the people of Ireland for making it possible. 'Today we
are truly a nation of equals.' They spoke of how LGBT people now
belonged 'as full and equal citizens'.

When they finished speaking, they were both hoarse and emotional. Then the room erupted again to the tune of Snow Patrol's 'Just Say Yes', which the band had lent to Yes Equality as its official campaign anthem. The HQ team came up and the stage wobbled as Yes Equality danced with joy.

Formalities over, Brian took the opportunity to change and shower in Gráinne's hotel room – with Gráinne's grandson Harry running around in his nappy, trying to charm poor Brian, who didn't realise he would be sharing his changing quarters with a twenty-month-old baby. His parents Conor Irwin and Ciara Travers had brought him along to witness the historic event. Brian and Harry played a game of hide and seek in the cupboard under the TV and as always, the laughter of a child brought ease after the tensions of the day.

As the evening moved into night and the crowd moved into the bar of the hotel, a request came through for the Yes Equality leaders to make an appearance in Pantibar.

Gráinne went off to change her dress and shoes and freshen up for the second jaunt into Dublin city centre. Noel, Cathy and Mark Garrett tagged along, each with their partners. If there was ever a night for a first visit to a gay night club, this was it. Séamus Dooley and Karl Hayden, still busy in his capacity as campaign videographer, also travelled. The entire north quay near Pantibar on Capel Street was cordoned off because of the crowd. Bouncers had to clear a path for Brian, Gráinne and the others. When they finally made it inside, speeches about the referendum had to wait. They had arrived at the denouement of the other very important count that day – the country by country jury votes for the Eurovision Song Contest. That spectacle could not be interrupted, no matter what had been won or lost in Ireland that day. The atmosphere was tense because Russia, not a popular country for its stance on homosexuality, was in the lead for a while, but was thankfully overtaken by Sweden.

At one stage Noel's considerable bulk was blocking the view of the TV screen for patrons in one corner of the bar and there were shouts of 'get the hell out of the way', but when someone nearby told them who the visitor was, there were hushed apologies of 'Oh, Noel Whelan;

oh that's no problem.' Brian later relayed the story to illustrate how the dour pundit had, for one day at least, become a gay icon.

When the Eurovision was over, Bráinne delivered another short speech of thanks to raucous cheers, noting that they were speaking from the same spot where they had welcomed the Constitutional Convention's decision to recommend a referendum just over two years earlier.

Afterwards, the Yes Equality crew slipped out the back door for a quieter drink in the nearby Morrison Hotel; they finished off the day with their first full glass of bubbly, this time chilled. Then they each went their separate ways – Noel and Sinead strolled across the noisy happy streets to get the Luas to Ranelagh, Brian was wrecked and took a taxi to Ringsend and Gráinne took a cab to rejoin Patricia who told her she would have a pot of tea waiting.

In the days that followed, the effect of this Irish referendum result would reverberate around the world. The large popular vote put the lie to the suggestion that marriage equality was somehow a policy concocted and enforced by elites. There were prompt calls in the parliaments of Germany and Australia for the same equality in their laws. Closer to home, there would be many anecdotes to illustrate the impact in Ireland itself, from the big things to the little ones, such as talk of children taking stories of the happy referendum weekend to school on Monday morning for Nuacht an Lá; of adults feeling they now had the freedom to hold hands in public with the person they loved.

That was all to come. In the early hours of Sunday morning, however, Yes Equality volunteers everywhere knew as they retired that it had been a Saturday like no other. It was the end of an extraordinary campaign involving thousands of extraordinary activists. They had helped the Irish people do something truly wonderful. They had not just changed the Constitution, they had changed the country.

CHAPTER 11

Truly a Nation
of Equals

Remarks by Gráinne Healy and Brian Sheehan on behalf of Yes Equality welcoming the result of Ireland's marriage equality referendum, 23rd May 2015.

'Today, we are more truly a nation of equals. The people of Ireland have exercised their constitutional right and by direct vote they have said an emphatic "Yes" to Equality. We now join twenty other countries where same-sex marriage has been made possible. We are the first country in the world to do so by a vote of the people.

This referendum was all about belonging – Irish lesbian and gay citizens had to ask the Irish people if they too can belong to Ireland and belong in Ireland. In their deep generosity the Irish people have said "Yes"– Yes, we belong. Today's result means that having been "branded and isolated" for decades, each lesbian and gay person knows now that they too belong in Ireland, as full, equal citizens.

It means more. It means that lesbian and gay couples belong to each other in a rich, new and profound way. That lesbian and gay parents belong anew to their children, and their children to them. And that mothers and fathers can now rest assured that their lesbian and gay children belong in the same way as all their children.

It means that all of us – lesbian, gay, bi-sexual, trans, straight, family members, friends, colleagues, allies, voters – belong equally to the Irish national family.

To the Irish people, to those who voted "Yes", you have done something that should make you forever proud. Do not forget this moment, this moment when you were your best self, when you chose to make your mark for an Ireland that could be a better and fairer place.

And to those who did not yet vote with us, we hope that, as lesbian and gay couples marry, you will see that we seek only to add to the happiness and the security of the diverse Irish national family.

While today is a day for celebration, it is only right that we should remember those who over the years were deprived of the opportunity that this "Yes" brings, those who were deprived of a fundamental human right.

We should remember the many lives blighted by shame, lives lived in loneliness and isolation, lives lost to hostility and fear. No longer should men and women have to hide a part of themselves from others and even from themselves, deprived of the opportunity to love and be loved.

We should remember too and honour those who took the first brave and lonely steps that led us to this day: those who pointed out the discrimination, the inequality, the segregation; those who refused – often at great personal cost – to be silenced or intimidated by the voices of intolerance; those who fought for equality, inclusion and recognition. They laid the foundations for today's transformative and historic change.

And there can be no doubt that this campaign for marriage equality has indeed been transformative. It has given LGBT people in Ireland permission to love ourselves and come out more comfortably and completely, some for the first time ever. It has generated a discussion and awareness among Irish people about equality and diversity and fairness – a discussion and awareness that will now flourish and grow.

While we know much remains to be done, today has been a turning point, one that should allow all lesbian and gay people in Ireland to fulfil their true potential – in family, in love, in life.

Now we can all begin to work together to change the lived experience of being LGBT. We can work together towards a day when any two people who love one another can feel fully safe expressing that love; when two people can, unremarked, walk down the street hand in hand. We can work together to ensure that young LGBT people in Ireland discover their identity in an atmosphere of support, affirmation and belonging.

This touching – this uplifting – outcome belongs to the Irish people. When the once-in-a-generation opportunity to make this landmark change was put before us, we grasped that opportunity with a resounding "Yes".

Today's result belongs to you. Be forever proud of what you have done.

Today's result belongs to the many thousands of volunteers who spent days and weeks standing on streets, knocking on doors, engaging their communities and neighbours in countless conversations about equality and belonging and love.

Today's result belongs to the people who shared their personal stories, laying bare the heartbreak, the loneliness, and the lost potential; touching hearts and minds; making it all but impossible for others to ignore the personal anguish and unnecessary pain inflicted by innate inequality on our gay citizens, and its impact on so many lives. The Irish people have now swept that world away.

Today's result belongs to the people who ran marathons, the people who baked cakes, the people who sold badges and t-shirts in every village and town to raise much-needed funds so that we could run a positive and constructive information campaign.

Today's result belongs to all of us – and together we can now move forward with our lives enriched and rejoice in the fact that we are on the right side of history, in a new nation of equals.

We will now add to our Constitution these seventeen words: "Marriage may be contracted in accordance with law by two persons without distinction as to their sex." With these words, we make it possible for our gay citizens to marry the person they love.

As our former President, Iar-Uachtarán Mary McAleese, said last week, our gay children will now be able to know the joy and peace and comfort of being part of a loving married couple fully recognised at the highest level our country can offer.

The Irish people have shown their compassion. They have shown profound and touching generosity, humanity and wisdom. They have made a historic change. The majority said one simple word; for a minority, that word means everything.

This movement saw a group of ordinary citizens undertake an extraordinary venture. With their might and grace, these people have given their hearts and souls to make marriage inclusive for all citizens. We are so proud of these people and of what they have helped to achieve.

Their achievement is no less than this: that today, we are true to the words of our Proclamation: "The Republic guarantees religious and civil liberty, equal rights and equal opportunities to all its citizens … cherishing all the children of the nation equally…"

Buíochas ó chroí.'

CHAPTER 12

A Message from Yes Equality Roscommon

The Following Statement was Posted on the Yes Equality Roscommon Facebook Page on Sunday 24th May 2015.

On this historic weekend, we wanted to say a few things. For the Yes Equality Roscommon volunteers, this has been an incredible experience. We have encountered heart-warming support throughout the whole campaign.

Unfortunately, we were small in number, and did not have the human resources to do, for example, large-scale canvasses as seen in other areas. We also suffered from a lack of support from local politicians. We watched in envy as well-known politicians in almost every other area in the country got publicly and deeply involved in the campaigns in their areas. Our multiple letters, texts and emails to our elected representatives went, for the most part, unanswered. There were two main exceptions to this, Maura Hopkins and Frank Feighan. We are forever grateful to them and will remember their help and support for a long time to come. We also won't forget the lack of support from other politicians when they ask for our votes.

However, we were thrilled and encouraged by the strong support we did encounter from the people of Roscommon. Individuals, businesses, families, parents, teenagers, grandparents – it was amazing to connect with so many wonderful people.

We recognise the work of our phenomenal volunteers – many of whom have dedicated every waking moment outside of their usual work to the campaign for the past several months. People from all walks of life, who shared a commitment to making Ireland a better place for everyone. Many canvassed in the rain, knocking on hundreds of doors per person.

We want to thank the extraordinary people at national YesEquality HQ in Dublin, who were a pleasure to work with and always available for us.

It's important to remember that 17,615 people in Roscommon-South Leitrim voted Yes to civil marriage equality (just 1,029 fewer than voted No). It's worth noting too, that many individual polling stations showed a majority for Yes. In a referendum, Ireland is one constituency, and every one of those Yes votes was counted and put towards the national result, an overwhelming majority in favour of equality. You made history.

To the 18,644 who voted No, and to others who voted No in every area of Ireland – Thank you for being part of this national conversation. We're certain that you'll see in due course that this necessary change, decided by the Irish people, is in everyone's best interests, including making Ireland a better place for you, should you, a family member or a friend of yours, come out as LGBT. As a result of this referendum, Ireland is already a kinder place.

Now, same-sex couples in Roscommon and around Ireland will be recognised as families through civil marriage, and be treated, under the law, as equal citizens in their own county and country. Their children will at last enjoy the protections of their parents' marriage. While LGBT kids will grow up knowing that their country cherishes them the same as their straight brothers and sisters.

This democratic decision of the people will change Ireland, for the better, forever, and has been and will continue to be heard around the world. We feel lucky to have been part of this change. Legal equality is here, and we hope that it will play a big part in eradicating discrimination and prejudice in society.

APPENDIX

Some of the Yes Equality Team

Yes Equality Executive Group Members:
Mark Kelly (ICCL), Kieran Rose (GLEN), Ailbhe Smyth (Marriage Equality) with Gráinne Healy and Brian Sheehan.

Yes Equality Advisory Group Members:
Denise Charlton, Séamus Dooley, Fergus Finlay, Mark Garrett, Gary Joyce, Mark Kelly (ICCL), Martin Mackin, Bride Rosney, Kieran Rose (GLEN), Ailbhe Smyth (Marriage Equality), Peter Ward, Senator Katherine Zappone, with Gráinne Healy, Cathy Madden, Brian Sheehan and Noel Whelan

Marriage Equality Board Members:
Board members have included: Carol Armstrong, Ross Golden-Bannon, Olive Braiden, Darina Brennan, Linda Cullen, Denise Charlton, Paula Fagan, Ronan Farren, Ann Louise Gilligan, Deirdre Hannigan, Orla Howard, Patrick Lynch, Anna McCarthy, Olivia McEvoy, Feargha Ní Bhroin, Kieran O'Brien, Clare O'Connell, Justine Quinn, Christopher Robson, Ailbhe Smyth, Judy Walsh, Katherine Zappone

GLEN Board Members:
Kieran Rose and Nathalie Weadick, Co-Chairs, Séamus Dooley, Arthur Leahy, Simon Nugent, Fergus Ryan, Margot Slattery, Muriel Walls. Previous board members have included: Ursula Barry, Eadaoinn Ní Chleirigh, Eoin Collins, Cathryn Mannion, Ciarán Ó Cuinn, Maura Molloy, Will Peters, Christopher Robson

ICCL Executive Board Members:
Siobhán Cummiskey and Niall Mulligan, Co-Chairs, Alan DP Brady, Claire Hamilton, Clare Naughton, Jonah Mudehwe, Deirdre Miller

Yes Equality HQ Team
Odhrán Allen, Paul Boylan, Tiernan Brady, Spence Christie, Karen Ciesielski, Vivienne Clarke, Niall Cremen, Andrew Deering, Mark Dempsey, Séamus Dooley, Craig Dwyer, Paula Fagan, Ross Flanagan, Niamh Griffin, Moninne Griffith, Marie Hamilton, Alan Hatton, Joe Hayes, Gráinne Healy, Suzanne Handley, Conor Hayes, Etain Hobson, Orla Howard, Kathleen Hunt, Andrew Hyland, Lisa Hyland, Sandra Irwin-Gowran, Walter Jayawardene, Yvonne Judge, Conor King, Natalie Lewendon, Cathy Madden, Mary McDermott, Jeanne McDonagh, Adam Murray, Simon Nugent, Stephen O'Hare, Ger O'Keefe, Eimear O'Reilly, Fergal O'Sullivan, Will Peters, Davin Roche, Brian Sheehan, Patrick Sweeney, Natalie Tennyson, Jon Weir, Noel Whelan

Shop: Glenna Benson, Leah Benson, Michael Byrne, Colm Carney, Gordon Cummins, Ciara Doyle, Paul Franey, Sean Franye, John Grogan, Aoibheana Hobson, Etain Hobson, Linda Kavanagh, Deirdre Kilbride, Gabriella Mastromatteo, Jim McElroy, Patricia Normanly, Hana O'Connor, Catriona O'Flynn, Ger O'Keefe, Steve Quinn, Brian Sherry, Joe Sullivan, Shona Sweeney, Justin Tallon, Jon Weir

Distribution: Kathy Dillon, Richard Johnson, Glen Hogarty, John McCarthy, Aine O'Connell, Matthew O'Dwyer, Lindsay Puddicombe, Stephen Quinn, Brian Sherry

Video Production: Shane Conaty, Karl Hayden, Conchubhair MacLochlainn, Stu Smith and Mariel O'Keefe

Yes Bus Team:
Evan Barry, Rowland Bennett, Paul Boylan, Michael Liam Browne, John Carmody, Brendan Carney, Aoife Clarke, Eva Rose Cullinan, Siofra Dempsey, Aisha Doody, Rebecca Doyle, Stephen Faherty, Darragh Finlay, Ross Flanagan, Luke Franklyn, Ross Golden-Bannon, Yolanda Gomez, Moninne Griffith, John Grogan, Aoibheana Hobson, Etain Hobson, Laura Hogan, Barbara Hughes, David Jameson, Emma Keaveney, Seb McAteer, Norah-Ide McAuliffe, Mary McDermott, Kieran McNulty, Maura Molloy, Owen Murphy, Áine O'Connell, Jessica O'Connor, Ger O'Keefe, Frank O'Malley, Martin O'Neill, Karl Ó Riain, Danielle O'Sullivan, Dan O'Toole, Shannon Phelan, Aoife Read, Ben Rogan, Joseph Ronan, Aoife Ryan Chrisensen, Laura Sheehan, Stephen Stafford, Anita Thoma, David Tynan, Jon Weir

Yes Equality Coordinators:
Dublin:
Dublin Bay North – Cian O'Callaghan and Ronan Burtenshaw
Dublin Bay South – John McNamara, Joanne Gilhooley, Justin McAleese
Dublin 1 & 3 (Dublin Central) – Gary Gannon
Dublin 7 – Olivia McEvoy
Balbriggan (Dublin Fingal) – Mary McGrath
Dublin 9/11 (Dublin North West) – Saoirse Brady and Des Egan
Dublin Fingal – Clodagh Murray and Conor Murphy
Dublin Mid-West – Karin Jonsson and Emily Smartt
Dublin North-East (Howth, Baldoyle, Sutton) – Ross Golden-Bannon
Dublin Rathdown/Stillorgan – Padraic Fleming and Gary Rooney
Dublin South-Central – Joan O'Connell
Dublin South-West – Darragh Genockey
Dublin West – Roderic O'Gorman, TJ Clare and Frances Byrne
Blackrock – Lynda Carroll
Dun Laoghaire – Hugo Mills

Leinster:
Yes Equality Carlow-Kilkenny – Enya Kennedy, Susie Faulkner and Mark Lacey
Yes Kilkenny – John Eardly
Kildare North & Kildare South – Vivian Cummins, Cris Pender, Ann Marie Lillis – Sarah Theloke, John Murphy and Gráinne Lawler
Laois – David Delaney
Offaly – Shane Scully and John Bennet
Longford-Westmeath – Declan Donohue, Donal MacAodh (Longford), Dee Bushell and Seámus Carey (Athlone), Shane Barkey and Deborah Stenson (Mullingar)
Louth – Bernadine Quinn, Anthony Kinahan and John Ruddy
Meath East and West – Conor Black, Maria O'Kane, Ronan Watters (Trim), David Farrelly (Kells) and Maurice Boland (Navan)
Wexford – Paddy Morris
Wicklow – Ian McGahon and William Quill and Gary Dempsey
West Wicklow – Sheila Quinn

Munster:
Clare – Orla Vaughan
All Cork constituencies – Ken Curtin and Una Feeley
Kerry – Rena Blake, Lisa Fingleton and Hilary Egan
Limerick – Dave Cuddihy and Jenny Hannon, Sharon McMeel, John James Hickey and Cillian Flynn
Tipperary – Thomas Ryan, Steven Glynn, Karen Eastwood and Damien McKelvey, Rowland Bennett, Debbie Hickey and Robert O'Donnell
Waterford – Micheal Hennessey, Alan O'Neill and Paul Knox

Connacht:
Galway West and East – Niall O'Tuathail, Sarah Clancy, Stephen Faherty and Regina Divilly, Kathy Walsh, Damien McGrath and Daniel Proctor
Mayo – Dora Murphy, Jean Cross, Marina Tuffy
Roscommon – Will Keane
Sligo-Leitrim – Kate Brennan-Harding, Niall Jordan and Anne Lewis

Ulster:
Cavan – Jane Connolly, Vincent Gilligan
Monaghan – Mary Gannon (Carrickmacross), Micheal Hughes (Monaghan Town)
Donegal – Noel Sharkey, Fionan Lynch and Tim Spalding

Yes Equality HQ Team Photo:
Back Row: Aoibheana Hobson, Steve Quinn, Paula Fagan, Darragh Finlay, Laura Sheehan, Connor King, Jon Weir, Niall Cremen, Craig Dwyer, Spence Christie, Stu Smith, Gabriella Mastromatteo, Leah Benson, Carol Armstrong, David Jameson, Aoife Ryan-Christensen

4th row: Karl Hayden, Etain Hobson, Adam May, Joe Hayes, Paul Boylan, Alan Hatton, Joanne Garvey, Karen Ciesielski, Eimear O'Reilly, Davin Roche, Gomez-The Dog, Lindsay Puddicombe, Kieran McNulty, Simon Nugent, Andrew Deering

3rd row: Nora Ide McAuliffe, Linda Cullen, Justine Quinn, Ross Golden-Bannon, Fergal O'Sullivan, Yvonne Judge, Ross Flanagan, Niamh Griffin, Fergus Ryan, Stephen O'Hare, Muriel Walls, Conchubhair Mac Loughlainn, Kathleen Hunt

2nd row: Hana O'Connor, Seámus Dooley, Ann Louise Gilligan, Senator Katherine Zappone, Cathy Madden, Olivia McEvoy, Anita Thoma, Daire Courtney, Orla Howard, Gráinne Courtney, Mary McDermott, Noel Whelan

Front Row: Sandra Irwin-Gowran, Patrick Sweeney, Andrew Hyland, Walter Jayawardene, Moninne Griffith, Gráinne Healy, Brian Sheehan, Kieran Rose, Ailbhe Smith, Tiernan Brady, Mark Kelly, Jeanne McDonagh

Notes

Chapter One

1. Full proceedings of the Constitutional Convention, except for the private sessions are available at https://www.youtube.com/channel/UCI1XuybPHA2o6E5AqUg8wdg. The Yes team included Muriel Walls and Tiernan Brady from GLEN, Stephen O'Hare from the ICCL and Moninne Griffith and Gráinne Healy from Marriage Equality, plus Conor Prendergast and Claire O'Connell from Believe in Equality, with others from each organisation operating behind the scenes.

Chapter Two

2. All social media analysis from Colin Oliver in http://www.CoconutCabin.ie"www.CoconutCabin.ie

Chapter Five

3. Groups included NXF, Outhouse, USI, GCN, Labour Party, LGBT Noize, Irish Trans Students Alliance, Sinn Féin LGBT, Red Ribbon Project, Dublin City Community Forum, Fine Gael LGBT, GAZE, Carlow Shout!, Running Amach, Vote With Us, Greenbow LGBT, Ógra Fianna Fáil, Dublin LGBTQ Pride, Labour Youth, Gaelick. com, Amnesty International, Dublin Devils FC, Dundalk Outcomers, LinC, National USI, Young Greens, DKIT LGBT society, Labour LGBT, Q Soc Trinity LGBT, Longford LGBT, Eile Magazine, BelongTo/LOOK, TENI.
4. Yes Equality Dublin Bay North, Dublin Bay South, Dublin 1 and 3, Dublin 7, Balbriggan, Dublin 9, Dublin 11, Fingal, Mid-West, North-West, Howth/Baldoyle/ Sutton, Dundrum-Rathdown, South Central, South West, West and Blackrock. See details of all Yes Equality groups nationwide in the appendix.

For further information on the developments that led to the referendum see YesEquality.ie, ICCL.ie, Marriageequality.ie and GLEN.ie

Index